PHUKET

TOP SIGHTS · LOCAL EXPERIENCES

ISABELLA NOBLE

Contents

Plan Your Trip 4

Wat Chalong Temple (p95)
VALERIYA KOVALEVA/SHUTTERSTOCK ©

Welcome to Phuket

Jade waves concealing rainbows of fish wash white-gold beaches beneath lushly jungled hills, beyond which lie temples and towns wrapped in Phuketian heritage: Phuket (ภูเก็ต), Thailand's dazzling largest island, is so diverse you may just forget to leave. The original Thai island getaway, Phuket may be much less undiscovered these days, but it still has its special allure.

Long-tail boats, Ao Phang-Nga (p136)

Top Experiences

Big Buddha

Phuket's 45m-high, Burmese-alabaster hilltop Buddha. **p76**

Laem Phromthep

Phuket's spectacular southernmost tip. **p90**

Old Phuket Town

Phuket's cultural capital; Sino-Portuguese architecture (pictured below). **p32**

Laem Phanwa

Jungled back-to-nature cape; quiet beaches. **p52**

Hidden Hôrng of Ao Phang-Nga

Phang-Nga's towering national-park limestone islets. **p136**

Ko Phi-Phi

Blonde beaches; jungle-covered limestone islets. **p14**

Diving in the Similan Islands

Some of Thailand's finest diving. **p138**

Eating

Beachside dining, bamboo shacks, heaving markets, sizzling street grills and smart restaurants. Phuket is a fantastic food destination, cooking up everything from terrific-value street eats to international fine dining – not to mention deliciously fresh seafood. Don't miss Phuket's Peranakan-style cooking, at its best in Phuket Town.

The Phuket Dining Scene

Phuket's dining options cater to all tastes and there's some fabulous food. Book ahead for top-end restaurants.

Street stalls Anywhere, at any time, for delicious Thai favourites.

Markets Phuket has plenty of markets with cheap, good meals.

Shophouse restaurants Semi-outdoor spaces dishing up Thai staples.

Restaurants From cheap-and-cheerful to elaborate and experimental, taking in everything from Thai to Italian.

Cafes Caffeine and brunch-style food; especially strong in Phuket Town.

Hotels Many of the island's finest restaurants are attached to hotels.

Best by Budget: $

Abdul's Roti Shop Phuket Town's favourite hotplate-fresh *roti*. (p42)

Kopitiam by Wilai Soak up the Old Town shophouse scene over flavour-bursting southern-Thai fare. (p42)

Pad Thai Shop *Pàt tai* with a serious kick, on Karon's roadside. (p74)

Lock Tien Sample signature Phuketian dishes. (p42)

Mee Ton Poe Plastic chairs and Hokkien noodles in Phuket Town. (p46)

Meena Restaurant No-fuss Thai staples overlooking Kamala's northern sands. (p105)

Best by Budget: $$$

Suay Choose **Cherngtalay** or **Phuket Town** for Noi Tammasak's signature fusion creations. (p119) (p42)

Bampot Imaginative European-style food and divine artisan cocktails (Cherngtalay). (p118)

Acqua Elaborate contemporary Italian cuisine from a Sardinian chef, just north of Patong. (p63)

GEET THEERAWAT/SHUTTERSTOCK ©

Ta Khai Phuketian classics are given a sophisticated makeover on Hat Tri-Trang. (p63)

Breeze Understated east-coast surrounds and European-inspired dishes starring Phuket produce. (p126)

Boathouse Top-end dining with sea breezes at Kata's finest restaurant. (p84)

Best Local Thai

Kopitiam by Wilai A Phuket Town shophouse setting for lip-smacking southern-Thai cooking. (p42)

One Chun Phuketian classics sizzled up in an atmospheric Old Town shophouse. (p42)

Raya One of Phuket Town's most established local-cuisine restaurants. (p45)

Tantitium Stylish design meets Phuketian specialities in a Sino-Portuguese Phuket Town building. (p45)

Pad Thai Shop Karon's favourite roadside food shack for terrific *pàt tai*. (p74)

Red Duck MSG-free Thai favourites on a Kata back-street. (p84)

Best Food Experiences

Phuket Food Tours Gastronomic wanders around Phuket Town. (p40)

Blue Elephant Cooking School Master Royal Thai specialities in a Phuket Town mansion. (p40)

Boathouse Cooking Class Fine-dining cookathons courtesy of Kata's swankiest restaurant. (p83)

Top Tip: Price Ranges

The following ranges refer to a main course.

$ less than 150B

$$ 150–350B

$$$ more than 350B

Drinking & Nightlife

Many travellers come to Phuket to party – whether that's at beachside bar shacks, sophisticated lounges, buzzing beach clubs or Patong's carnival of sin. It isn't all about dirt-cheap shots and go-go bars: Kata has mellow sand-side bars and Ao Bang Thao is classy-beach-club territory, while Phuket Town is an artisan coffee and cocktails hot spot.

Best Cocktails

Dibuk House The star of Phuket Town's blossoming handcrafted-cocktail scene. (p47)

Tantitium Expertly mixed, inventive artisan cocktails in a beautiful Sino-Portuguese Phuket Town setting. (p45)

Baba Nest Watch the sun sink over classic cocktails from Phuket's most fabulous sunset-watching bar. (p53)

Club No 43 A moody Phuket Town lounge serving imaginative, ambitious cocktails. (p48)

Bampot Arguably northern Phuket's best cocktails, in chic minimalist surrounds. (p118)

Best Cafes

Shelter Coffee Award-wining coffee and brunchy bites at this Phuket Town garden cafe. (p47)

Bookhemian One of the island's most fashionable cafes, on Phuket Town's Th Thalang. (p47)

Project Artisan Creative Cherngtalay space for cocktails, craft beers and gorgeous, locally sourced breakfasts. (p119)

Gallery Cafe Pinky's popular, artsy creation has pick-me-up breakfasts and has several branches across the island. (p46)

DouBrew All about expertly poured coffee on Phuket Town's prettiest street. (p48)

Best Clubs

Catch Beach Club The place to be seen on beautiful Ao Bang Thao. (p117)

Illuzion A packed-out dance floor and countless bars at Patong's top mega-club, on Th Bangla. (p67)

Timber Hut This low-key, split-level pub-club is a long-standing Phuket Town favourite. (p48)

XANA Beach Club Cabana cocktail lounging by day; pounding DJ sets by night, on Ao Bang Thao. (p118)

Café del Mar Feel the Ibizan vibes at Kamala's newest beach club. (p105)

Plan Your Trip Drinking & Nightlife

Best LGBT+

Phuket Pride Week One of Southeast Asia's best LGBT+ Pride celebrations, centred on Patong. (p68)

Zag Club Fabulous cabarets take over Patong's favourite LGBT+ bar every night. (p67)

Boat Bar Phuket's original gay bar-club, with nightly cabarets, in Patong. (p67)

My Way One of Patong's earliest gay bars, for sparkling cabaret. (p67)

Best Laid-Back Bars

Ska Bar A chilled-out reggae bar tucked into southern Hat Kata Yai. (p86)

Art Space Cafe & Gallery This friendly, eccentric Kata hangout mixes drinks, art, veggie meals and tattoos. (p86)

After Beach Bar Perched high above Hat Kata Noi, a mellow Bob Marley–fuelled bar-restaurant. (p86)

Beach Bar Low-key luxe beachfront cocktail bar on Hat Pansea. (p112)

NY Beach Republic Beachy lounge bar bringing nightlife to Hat Nai Yang. (p135)

Reggae Bar Rawai's easygoing Rasta party pad. (p99)

Best Entertainment

Bebop The island's top jazz musicians flaunt their skills at this moody Phuket Town bar. (p49)

Phuket Simon Cabaret This sensationally over-the-top cabaret is the quintessential Patong experience. (p67)

Galaxy Boxing Stadium Watch competitors battle it out with *moo·ay tai* (Thai boxing) bouts. (p68)

Patong Pub & Grub Crawl Hit Patong's harmless enough pubs. (p56)

Beaches

Of Phuket's 8.4 million visitors, 99% zip straight to the beach. Flashy ever-more-developed strands mingle with a few hidden paradises along the island's 50km coast, where clear aqua waters wash gold-blonde sands fringed by lush jungle. A big clean-up (p146) has swept through since 2014, reducing the 'services' clogging up the sand.

Which Beach is for You?

Most visitors make a beeline for the west coast's established, social tourist magnets of Hat Kata (p83), Hat Karon (p73) and (seedier) Hat Patong (p62): long sandy swathes lined with resorts, restaurants, bars and every other facility you could dream of. If you'd prefer a more peaceful, secluded vibe, hunt down rocky coves off nondescript coastal roads between the main beaches, or head to Phuket's less

touristed northwest coast, where Hat Mai Khao (p131), Hat Nai Yang (p131) and Hat Nai Thon (p131) are protected by Sirinat National Park (p132). For five-star sparkle without the bustle, seek out Hat Surin (p109) and Ao Bang Thao (p114). In the far south, Rawai has a mellow vibe and is home to beautiful Hat Nai Han (p93).

Best for Relaxation

Hat Surin Stunning back-to-nature white-gold strand. (p109)

Hat Pansea Dreamy sunsets and creamy west-coast sands. (p109)

Hat Nai Han Mellow vibes meet bleach-blonde sand near Rawai. (p93)

Hat Nai Thon A peaceful sweep with few distractions. (p131)

Hat Mai Khao Phuket's tranquil longest beach. (p131)

Hat Nai Yang Nature and tourism commune on this laid-back national-park strand. (p131)

Best Hidden Sands

Hat Ya Nui An easygoing sapphire Rawai cove with glorious sunsets. (p93)

ALEKSANDAR TODOROVIC/SHUTTERSTOCK ©

Banana Beach Clamber down the jungle-clad hillside to a boulder-studded beach. (p132)

Ao Sane A small, tucked away Rawai favourite. (p94)

Best for Families

Hat Kata Two fun-filled crescent bays with good facilities. (p83)

Hat Nai Han At the southern tip of the island, with a low-key feel. (p93)

Hat Kamala Calm waters and good snorkelling. (p103)

Best for Water Sports

Rawai Kitesurfing central on east-coast beaches. (p95)

Hat Kata Yai Excellent surfing, SUP and dive schools. (p83)

Hat Kamala Surf breaks and snorkelling. (p103)

Hat Patong Diving, parasailing, jet skis and more. (p62)

Hat Nai Yang Surfing and kitesurfing during the monsoon. (p131)

Best Party Vibe

Hat Bang Thao Beautiful 8km sweep of sand with glitzy beach clubs. (p117)

Hat Kamala Beach club scene mixed with a village atmosphere. (p103)

Hat Patong Phuket's free-for-all party capital. (p62)

Worth a Trip: Natai

Just 26km north of Phuket's airport, the increasingly popular luxury bolthole of **Natai** lies within easier reach of Phuket than parts of Phuket itself. There's little out here, apart from some of southern Thailand's most exclusive restaurants and hotels and a delicious broad blonde beach that disappears into turquoise waters.

Water Sports

Diving is Phuket's star water activity, but you can also take to the water for snorkelling, kitesurfing, sea kayaking, yachting and surfing. November to April is the season for diving and snorkelling, while the monsoon is best for surfing and kitesurfing off the west coast. Weather permitting, however, activities run year-round.

CHAINARONG PHRAMMANEE/SHUTTERSTOCK ©

Diving & Snorkelling

One-day, two-dive trips to nearby sites start at around 3800B; Open Water Diver certification costs 11,000B to 21,000B for three days' instruction. From Phuket, you can join liveaboard diving expeditions to the Similan Islands (p138). The best diving months are November to April; some dive sites may close during the May-to-October monsoon.

Snorkelling isn't wonderful off Phuket proper, though gear (200B per day) and snorkel tours are available in most resort areas.

Kitesurfing & Surfing

One of the world's fastest-growing sports, kitesurfing is among Phuket's big addictions. The best kitesurfing spots are Hat Nai Yang (p131) from May to October and Rawai (p89) from November to March. Reliable outfitters are affiliated with the International Kiteboarding Organisation (www.ikointl.com). Phuket is also an under-the-radar surf destination.

Sea Kayaking & SUP

Several Phuket-based companies offer canoe tours of spectacular Ao Phang-Nga (p137). A day paddle (around 4000B per person) includes meals, equipment and boat transfer. Stand-up paddleboarding (SUP; 400B per hour) is available from most beaches; there are good tours, too.

ADRIAN BAKER/SHUTTERSTOCK ©

Best Diving & Snorkelling

Sea Fun Divers Liveaboard Similans trips, PADI courses and day trip dives around Phuket and Phi-Phi; keen, professional instructors. (p60)

Sea Bees This long-standing dive operation offers day trips to Ko Phi-Phi, SSI certification and Similans liveaboards. (p60)

Sunrise Divers The island's biggest liveaboard agent (Similan and Surin Islands); day trips to Ko Phi-Phi and Similans. (p74)

Dive Asia Hits the standard Phi-Phi day dives, plus PADI courses and liveboards

to the Similan and Surin Islands. (p74, 85)

Rumblefish Adventure Kata based boutique school with the usual day trips, liveaboards and PADI courses, plus a guesthouse. (p85)

Best Kitesurfing & Surfing

Kiteboarding Asia Thailand-wide operator with branches in Rawai and Hat Nai Yang. (p93)

Kite Zone Rawai-based kitesurfing specialist. (p93)

Hat Kamala Popular surf spot May to October. (p103)

Hat Karon Monsoon-season surf lessons. (p74)

Hat Kata Classes and surfing kit hire April to November. (p85)

Best Sea Kayaking & SUP

John Gray's Seacanoe The island's star operator; day trips and multiday kayaking and camping trips to Ao Phang-Nga and Khao Sok. (p137)

Nautilus Dive & Surf Shop Specialising in 'everything that's in the water', based on southern Hata Kata Yai. (p81)

Cultural Sights

THAISIGN/SHUTTERSTOCK ©

It can be tricky to tear yourself away from the beach, but Phuket's cultural attractions are very rewarding. Phuket Town is the island's cultural heart, but each area has its own flavour. The Burmese-alabaster Big Buddha keeps watch over the south, while Buddhist temples, Chinese shrines and elegant mosques lie sprinkled across the island.

Best Museums

Phuket Thaihua Museum
A Phuket Town beauty filled with exhibits on Phuket's Chinese and tin-mining history. (p38)

Chinpracha House This beautifully preserved Sino-Portuguese Phuket Town mansion is one for antique or architecture lovers. (p38)

Best Architecture

Old Phuket Town Phuket's most architecturally fascinating streets, packed with Sino-Portuguese shophouses and mansions. (p32)

Soi Romanee Phuket Town's finest historical street. (p35)

Best Religious Sites

Big Buddha One of the world's largest Buddhas towers 45m high atop Phuket's Nakkerd Hills; consider hiking up! (p76)

Wat Chalong A major Phuket temple with 36 golden Buddhas and a pink-washed *chedi*. (p95)

Wat Phra Thong Thalang's serene temple of the half-buried Golden Buddha. (p125)

Shrine of the Serene Light Check out Taoist etchings and vaulted ceilings at this incense-cloaked Phuket Town shrine. (p38)

Worth a Trip: Wat Sireh

Perched on the highest point of Ko Sireh, 5km east of Phuket Town, **Wat Sireh** (วัดบ้านเกาะสิเหร่; Th Sireh; admission free; ⌚daylight hours) is a sun-faded, 60-year-old temple surrounded by dozens of gold-painted Buddhas, and is one of Phuket's most important religious sites. Inside is a massive reclining golden Buddha.

Shopping

Browsing the shops is a favourite pastime for visitors to Phuket. Surin and Bang Thao/Cherngtalay host beach-chic boutiques, while Surin, along with Phuket Town, also has intriguing art and antiques. You'll find more fashion stores in Phuket Town, with vintage gems and colourful local textiles. Keep an eye out for budget-friendly local markets.

BUTENKOV ALEKSEI/SHUTTERSTOCK ©

Best Fashion

Chandra Glam island-chic boutique in **Surin** and **Cherngtalay** (p112, 121)

Ranida Vintage-inspired women's couture meets antiques gallery in Phuket Town. (p50)

Pink Flamingo Hand-painted murals adorn a reimagined Phuket Town building stocked with Bali-born fashion. (p50)

Boat Avenue High-end al-fresco Cherngtalay shopping complex. (p121)

Baru Chic breezy beachwear in Karon. (p75)

Ban Boran Textiles Colourful fabrics, fashion and acces-sories from across Southeast Asia. (p50)

Best Markets & Malls

Walking St A busy Sunday-afternoon market takes over Phuket Town's colourful Th Thalang. (p50)

Jung Ceylon Patong's glossy international-brand shopping centre. (p69)

Central Festival Queen of Phuket's malls; near Phuket Town. (p51)

Weekend Market Phuket's version of Bangkok's massive Chatuchak market. (p51)

Best Art & Antiques

Oriental Fine Art Surin's outstanding, museum-wor-thy collection of traditional Southeast Asian art. (p113)

Drawing Room Bold, abstract contemporary artwork in Phuket Town. (p50)

Raanboonpitak Impressive treasure trove of antiques in Patong. (p68)

Soul of Asia Asian antiques and original art from a Surin collector. (p113)

Best Beauty & Wellness

Lemongrass House All-natural health and beauty products from the island's favourite home-grown brand; branches in **Surin** and **Karon**. (p75, 112)

Oldest Herbs Shop Century-old family-run outlet for Chinese herbal remedies. (p50)

Spas & Massage

Once you're done sun-soaking, diving, paddling or partying, Phuket offers some fabulous pampering. Whether you splurge or save, prepare to be soaked, scrubbed, massaged and wrapped into beach bliss at spas all across the island. Brave a muscle-pounding classic Thai massage or go for a soothing aloe vera wrap and floral steam bath.

TONGRO IMAGES INC/GETTY IMAGES ©

Best Indulgent Spas

Cool Spa Fruit-infused treatments in a sensational, luxurious Laem Phanwa location; don't miss the **Baba Nest** bar. (p53)

Mala Spa Organic products and expert-led massages, wraps and more at Kamala's fantasy-world **Keemala**. (p103)

Coqoon Spa A suspended 'nest' suite, a stunning rainforest backdrop and five-star service in Hat Nai Yang. (p132)

Infinite Luxury Spa This ultra-modern spa combines traditional techniques with high-tech treatments. Ah, the anti-jetlag pod... (p83)

SALA Spa Sleek massage rooms in private pebbled courtyards on Hat Mai Khao. (p133)

Banyan Tree Spa Highly regarded top-end Bang Thao resort spa for Thai and Indian therapies. (p117)

Mom Tri's Spa Royale Celebrated Kata spa starring organic products. (p83)

Sun Spa Signature therapies at a glossy Surin address. (p110)

Baray Spa Treatments among waterfalls, canals and gardens. (p83)

Best Affordable Spas

Thai Carnation A local-style spa steal in upmarket Ao Bang Thao. (p118)

Raintree Spa Excellent-value Phuket Town spa in tranquil tropical gardens. (p40)

Oasis Spa Classic surrounds plus Thai and Ayurvedic treatments in Kamala. (p104)

Atsumi Detox retreat with fasting, massages, yoga and a pool, in Rawai. (p94)

The Spa Soothing Karon spa among lovely tropical gardens. (p73)

For Kids

While the seedier side of Thailand's sex industry is on show in Patong (we'd steer clear of it with kids), the rest of Phuket is fairly G-rated, with amusements galore. Due to animal-welfare concerns, we do not recommend Kamala's supposedly 'family-friendly' Phuket Fantasea (p104) or any of the island's many elephant rides (p149).

GINA SMITH/SHUTTERSTOCK ®

Best Wildlife Encounters

Phuket Elephant Sanctuary Feed, watch and walk with rescued pachyderms at this responsible sanctuary in the island's northeast. (pictured above, p127)

Soi Dog Meet Thailand's cats and dogs at this nonprofit animal-rescue foundation near Hat Mai Khao. (p132)

Phuket Gibbon Rehabilitation Project A tiny northeastern sanctuary that adopts captive gibbons in the hope they can re-enter the wild. (p125)

Phuket Aquarium Plenty of underwater surprises on Laem Phanwa, including tiger-striped catfish, reef sharks and a 600V electric eel. (p53)

Best Activities

Phuket Riding Club Trot through the jungle and along golden sands around Hat Mai Khao. (p133)

Kiteboarding Asia Older kids can kitesurf the Andaman's waves in Rawai and Hat Nai Yang. (p93)

Khao Phra Thaew Royal Wildlife & Forest Reserve Head out into this protected park full of waterfalls and singing gibbons. (p126)

Nam Tok Bang Pae It's a short shaded jungle walk to these national-park falls for a swim. (p126)

Top Tip: Phuket Wake Park

Buzz Kathu's marvellous hill-backed lake on a wakeboard. **Phuket Wake Park** (📞 076 510151; www.phuketwakepark.com; 86/3 Mu 6, Th Vichitsongkram, Kathu; adult/child 2hr visit 950/450B, day pass 1600/800B; ⏰ 9am-6pm), mostly aimed at teenagers and older kids, offers rides in one-, two- or four-hour blocks, by the day or as lessons (1000B per hour). Board rental is available (from 300B), as are hotel transfers.

Four Perfect Days

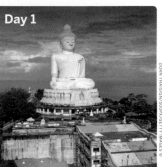

Day 1

Day 2

DORN THAISIGN/500PX/GETTY IMAGES ©

Beat the heat by whizzing (or hiking) up to **Big Buddha** (p76) early. Then grab lunch at **Red Duck** (p84) in Kata, followed by lazing on **Hat Kata Yai** (p83). Alternatively, head south to casuarina-fringed **Hat Nai Han** (p93) and Rawai's low-key cafes. As the sun starts to sink, wind your way to **Laem Phromthep** (p90). Drop down to mellow **Nikita's** (p99) on Hat Rawai or swing by Kata's **After Beach Bar** (p86).

Splash out on beachside dinner at Kata's romantic **Boathouse** (p84) or, in Rawai, at luscious **Rum Jungle** (p95). Round the evening off with cocktails at Kata's beachfront **Ska Bar** (p86).

Time to explore history-rich east-coast Phuket Town. Find breakfast at **Shelter Coffee** (p47) or **Abdul's Roti Shop** (p42), before meandering around the Sino-Portuguese Old Town (p32), including pastel-tastic **Soi Romanee** (p32).

Lunch Phuket-style at **Kopitiam by Wilai** (p42), **One Chun** (p42) or **Raya** (p45), then pick up a latte at **Bookhemian** (p47) or **DouBrew** (p48) and scour boutiques and galleries like **Ranida** (p50) and **Drawing Room** (p50).

Stay for the evening with fusion sensations at **Suay** (p42) or Phuket classics at **Tu Kab Khao** (p43) and **Tantitium** (p45). Then party local-style: **Bebop** (p49) jazz, **Dibuk House** (p47) cocktails, and pub-club **Timber Hut** (p48).

Day 3

Wake up and smell the espresso at Surin's **Bocconcino** (p110) or **Phuket Coffee Lab** (p111), then wander the boutiques: beach-chic **Chandra** (p112), all-natural **Lemongrass House** (p112), original **Oriental Fine Art** (p113). Spend the rest of the morning on **Hat Surin** (p109) or **Hat Pansea** (p109).

Next, head south to **Hat Kamala** (p103) for beach-club bliss at **Café del Mar** (p105) and surf/SUP sessions. Refuel at **Meena Restaurant** (p105) or **Isaan Popeye Thai Food** (p105), before visiting the **Tsunami Memorial** (p103).

If budget allows, escape into the hills for a **spa treatment** and meal at magical **Keemala** (p103). Otherwise, dine at **Blue Manao** (p104).

Day 4

Breakfast at **Monkeypod** (p126) en route to the **Phuket Elephant Sanctuary** (p127). Squeeze in the **Phuket Gibbon Rehabilitation Project** (p125), relishing the beauty of **Khao Phra Thaew Royal Wildlife & Forest Reserve** (p126), then, time permitting, seek out **Wat Phra Thong** (p125).

Travel west to Cherngtalay for late lunch at uberchic **Catch Beach Club** (p119) on **Hat Bang Thao** (p117). Pop inland for a treatment at **Thai Carnation** (p118) or **Banyan Tree Spa** (pictured above; p117) or shopping at **Boat Avenue** (p121).

Post-sunset, will it be **Suay** (p119), **Bampot** (p118), **Siam Supper Club** (p120) or **Pesto** (p119) for dinner? Finally, swing by **Project Artisan** (p119).

Need to Know

For detailed information, see Survival Guide p142

Currency
Thai baht (B)

Language
Thai

Visas
Not generally required
for stays of up to 30
days when arriving
by air.

Money
ATMs widely available;
credit and debit cards
accepted in some
hotels and restaurants
(usually high end).

Mobile Phones
Prepaid local SIM cards
are readily available at
shopping centres and
convenience stores
such as 7-Eleven, and
work with any unlocked
GSM phone.

Time
Indochina Time (GMT
plus seven hours)

Tipping
Not generally expected,
but appreciated. Most
upmarket eateries add
a 10% service charge
to bills.

Daily Budget

Budget: Less than 1000B

Dorm bed: 300–700B

Budget private room: 600–1000B

Street food or market meal: 30–200B

Sŏrng·tăa·ou (minibus) or motorcycle taxi trip: 25–50B

Midrange: 1000–3000B

Guesthouse or hotel room: 1200–3000B

Meal with drinks: 250–700B

Spa treatment: 300–1500B

Top end: More than 3000B

Room in resort or boutique hotel: from 3000B

Fine dining with wine: 500–1500B

One-day, two-dive trip: 3800–4400B

Car hire: 1200B

Useful Websites

Go Phuket (www.gophuket.net) Travel guide
and blog from island expat Lana Willocks.

Jamie's Phuket (www.jamiesphuketblog.com)
Insider's blog by a long-time Phuket expat.

Lonely Planet (www.lonelyplanet.com/thai
land/phuket-province) Destination information,
hotel bookings, traveller forum and more.

Phuket 101 (www.phuket101.net) Photo-led
blog with expat Willy Thuan's stellar Phuket tips.

Phuket News (www.thephuketnews.com) Up-
to-date news, with cultural/tourism coverage.

Phuket.com (www.phuket.com) A sophisticated
digest of information and recommendations.

Arriving in Phuket

✈ Phuket International Airport

Most visitors arrive into **Phuket International Airport** (www.phuketairport online.com), 30km northwest of Phuket Town.

Metered taxis (most convenient) await just outside international arrivals, and shouldn't cost over 700B to anywhere on Phuket.

Twelve daily airport buses (www.airportbus phuket.com) run to/from Phuket Town's Bus Terminal 1 (Th Phang-Nga; 100B, one hour), leaving the airport 8am to 8.30pm and Phuket Town 6am to 6.30pm. **Phuket Smart Bus** (📞086 306 1257; www.phuket smartbus.com; 50-170B) links the airport with west-coast beaches and Rawai (50B to 170B, hourly 6am to 8.15pm).

Minivans run to some west-coast beaches (200B).

Getting Around

Local Phuket transport is famously terrible, though things are slowly improving. Taxis remain heavily overpriced.

🚗 Car & Motorcycle

Car rental (from 1000B per day) and scooter hire (250B per day) are easily arranged.

🚕 Taxi

You'll find taxi ranks in beach towns; most travel agents arrange drivers. Metered taxis (more reasonably priced) remain hard to find, apart from at Phuket's airport. Taxi app Grab is handy (p147).

🚌 Bus

Phuket Smart Bus links Rawai, airport and west-coast beaches.

Sŏrng·tǎa·ou & Túk-Túk

Slow, inexpensive *sŏrng·tǎa·ou* (passenger pick-up trucks) run between Phuket Town and the beaches; *túk túk* (pronounced dúk dúk; motorised transport) charters are handy (but pricey).

Phuket Regions

Ao Bang Thao & Cherngtalay (p115)
A stunning 8km stretch of blinding-white sand with some top-end resorts and beach clubs, plus outstanding restaurants tucked inland.

Hat Surin (p107)
Sophisticated Hat Surin blends beach bliss with a villagey vibe, boutiques and natural beauty.

Hat Kamala (p101)
Keep things laid-back, with a gold-white beach and a mix of tourism, surfing, beach clubs and local village atmosphere.

Hat Patong (p55)
Go-go bars, raunchy cabaret, nightclubs and hedonism: Patong is Phuket's 'sin city'.

Hat Karon (p71)
Fun-loving Karon lures beach lovers with its gorgeous long white-sand stretch, and opens up the hike to Big Buddha.

Hat Kata (p79)
Perfect for families with high-end dining, beachside bars, diving, spas and beaches.

Phuket International Airport

Northern Beaches
(p129)
A trio of beauties that
have so far managed to
escape the full effects of
Phuket's tourism boom.

Northeastern Phuket
(p123)
Hike to waterfalls and
meet singing gibbons
and rescued elephants
in Khao Phra Thaew
Royal Wildlife & Forest
Reserve, then explore
serene temples.

Phuket Town **(p31)**
Sino-Portuguese
architecture; Chinese
Taoist shrines; boutique
guesthouses; booming
coffee, cocktail and art
scenes; lively local bars .

*Old
Phuket
Town*

*Big
Buddha*

Rawai **(p89)**
Discover spectacular
viewpoints, chilled-out
bars and cafes, secluded
sands in hidden pockets
and an un-Phuket-like
mellow vibe in breezy,
low-key Rawai.

*aem
hromthep*

Explore
Phuket

Wat Chalong (p95) CONNOR STRZELEWICZ/SHUTTERSTOCK ©

Explore ◉
Phuket Town

A colourful blend of cultural influences, the Old Town is a testament to Phuket's history, but it's also the island's hipster heart. Century-old hôrng tăa·ou (shophouses) are being restored, vibrant street art is popping up amid distinctive Sino-Portuguese architecture, and Phuket Town remains a wonderfully refreshing cultural break from the island's beaches.

The Short List

○ **Old Phuket Town Architecture (p33)** Wandering between Sino-Portuguese shophouses and hunting down ancient Chinese shrines.

○ **Cafe Culture (p47)** Seeking out the island's finest coffee beans at creative cafes around town.

○ **Local Cooking (p42)** Sampling Phuket's specialities; don't miss the famous roti shops on Th Thalang.

○ **Cocktail Time (p47)** Drinking in the blossoming crafted-cocktail scene.

○ **Boutique Bliss (p50)** Scouting for antiques, vintage fashion, experimental art and secondhand books.

Getting There & Around

🚗 To/from the airport 550B; Patong 500B; Kata 600B; Surin 700B.

🚌 Bright-orange airport buses: 12 times daily (100B, one hour, 6am to 8.30pm). Local bus from Bus Terminal 1 to Patong (30B, 7am to 5pm).

Sŏrng·tăa·ou Bus-sized pick-up trucks between Th Ranong and beaches (30B to 40B, 30 minutes to 1½ hours, 7am to 6pm).

Phuket Town Map on p36

Sino-Portuguese shopfronts (p32) KEVIN HELLON/SHUTTERSTOCK ©

Top Experience 📷
Old Phuket Town

Once the beating heart of the island's 19th- and 20th-century tin-mining industry, the atmospheric Old Town has undergone major restorations in the last decade, with its historic Sino-Portuguese buildings vibrantly repainted, new cafes, bars and guesthouses appearing and, more recently, fresh street art adding pops of colour. It's still a real slice of multifaceted Phuket history and local life.

◉ MAP P36, D4

Sŏrng·tăa·ou Between Th Ranong and Phuket's beaches (30B to 40B, 7am to 6pm)

🚌 Local bus from Bus Terminal 1 to Patong (30B, 7am to 5pm).

🚗 Sample rates: Patong 500B, Surin 700B.

Sino-Portuguese Architecture

Born from combining Chinese and European styles, Phuket Town's elaborate Sino-Portuguese architecture peaked in the early 20th century at the height of the tin-mining boom.

Some of the most beautifully restored buildings line Soi Romanee (p35), originally Phuket Town's red-light district, and Th Thalang, the Old Town's lively main street. There are plenty more to be unearthed along Ths Dibuk, Baowarat, Ranong, Phang-Nga, Krabi and Rassada. Prime examples are the Standard Chartered Bank (p35), the old post office building (p35), Chinpracha House (p38) and Phra Pitak Chinpracha Mansion (p35). Hidden among all these are important Chinese shrines thick with incense.

Phuketian Cuisine

Estimates suggest that 70% of Phuket's population comes from Peranakan (Southeast Asian-Chinese) ancestry, and this rich heritage shines through in local Phuketian cuisine, which has its own distinctive flavours and specialities found only here in Thailand. Look for *mèe hokkien* (Hokkien noodles), dim sum, Chinese cookies and Muslim *roti*, as well as typical 'fusion' dishes like *lobha* (pork cheek and offal), *mŏo hong* (pepper-and-garlic-braised pork), *pàk miang* (kale-like leaves, often scrambled with eggs) and *gaang pôo* (crab-meat curry).

Crafted Coffee & Cocktails

Phuket Town's young entrepreneurs are busy experimenting with both coffee beans and personalised spirits, meaning the city is the island's best spot for highly original, Thai-inspired artisan cocktails and expertly poured espresso.

★ **Top Tips**

o Phuket Town is becoming increasingly popular with visitors and tour groups; swing by first thing or stay overnight to catch it at its most peaceful.

o Many of the best local breakfast places open and fill up from around 6am onwards; get there early.

o Despite widespread revamps, many of Phuket Town's Sino-Portuguese homes can only be admired from the outside; Chinpracha House (p38) is an exception.

✗ **Take a Break**

Stop for a caffeine-fuelled breather and a brunchy bite at prize-winning Shelter Coffee (p47).

Settle in for Phuketian specialities at converted shophouse Kopitiam by Wilai (p42).

Walking Tour 🥾

Phuket Town's Architectural Legacies

A world away from white-sand beaches, Phuket Town offers a rare insight into the island's fascinating history. This walk through its historic core leads you past the 19th-century architectural legacies, grandiose mansions and slender shophouses of the Baba people (also Peranakan or Straits-Chinese), weaving in a couple of historical museums.

Walk Facts

Start Phuket Thaihua Museum

End Memory at On On Hotel

Length 2.5km; two to three hours

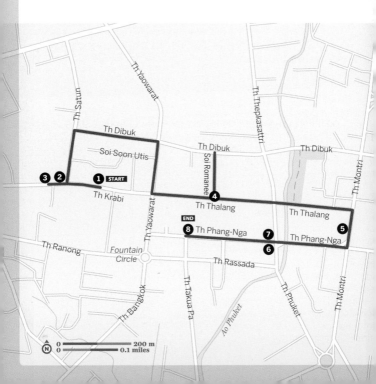

❶ Phuket Thaihua Museum

Start with the majestic **Phuket Thaihua Museum** (p38). Dating from 1934, this was the oldest Chinese school in Thailand and exhibits European-Sino-Thai architectural styles and local-life multimedia displays.

❷ Phra Pitak Chinpracha Mansion

Head west along Th Krabi and wander into the gardens overlooking the Th Satun junction, where the early-20th-century Phra Pitak Chinpracha Mansion has been immaculately restored as one of Phuket's finest Thai restaurants and cooking schools, **Blue Elephant** (p45).

❸ Chinpracha House

Immediately west, a muralled alley leads to beautiful **Chinpracha House** (p38), built in 1903 on tin-mining wealth. It's now a private home and museum, owned by the descendants of the original builder.

❹ Th Thalang & Soi Romanee

Stroll north along Th Satun and turn right (east) onto brightly painted Th Dibuk, then right (south) on Th Yaowarat next to the mural of Rama IX (Bhumibol Adulyadej; r 1946–2016), and left (east) on historical **Th Thalang**.

Just off Th Thalang is **Soi Romanee**, whose vividly restored Sino-Portuguese shophouses shimmer under Chinese paper lanterns.

❺ Old Post Office

Continue east along Th Thalang, crossing the canal, then turn right (south) on Th Montri, and you'll spot the old post office, a classic (if flaking) example of Sino-Portuguese architecture housing the **Phuket Philatelic Museum** (พิพิธภัณฑ์ตราไปรษณียากรภูเก็ต; admission free; 9am-5.30pm Tue-Sat).

❻ Standard Chartered Bank

Next, it's west along Th Phang-Nga to reach the renovated, yellow-washed **Standard Chartered Bank** (ธนาคารสแตนดาร์ดชาร์เตอร์ด; museum 9am-4.30pm Tue-Sun), in typical Sino-Portuguese style. Thailand's first local bank, it's now an erratically open museum showcasing Phuket's Baba culture, but best admired from outside.

❼ Thai Police Building

Directly opposite is the **Thai Police Building** (Th Phang-Nga; 9am-4.30pm Tue-Sun), restored in sun-yellow, with its police-cap roof and late-20th-century clock tower.

❽ Phuket's First Hotel

Head west again on Th Phang-Nga, passing restaurants within lovely old shophouses, to the smartly revamped **Memory at On On Hotel** (076 363700; www.thememoryhotel.com; d 1700-2350B;). Phuket's first hotel sprawls behind its gleaming-white Sino-Portuguese facade to terracotta-tiled patios, mosaic-floor halls and imposing wooden staircases.

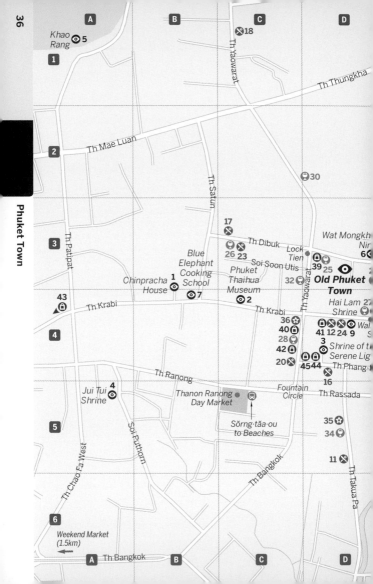

A **B** **C** **D**

Khao
Rang 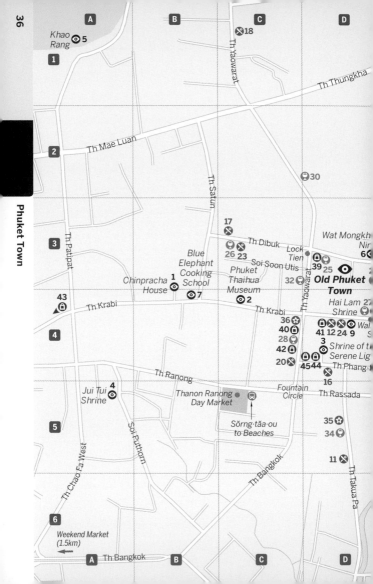5

1

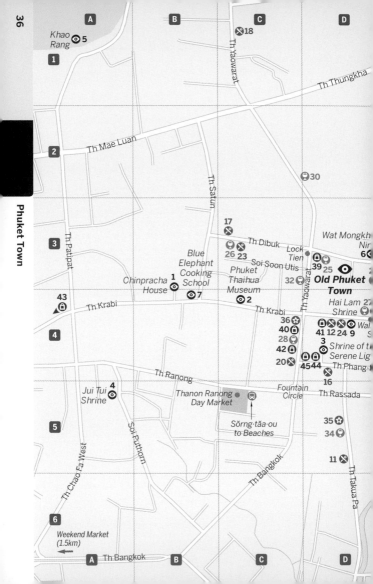18

Th Yaowarat

Th Thungkha

Th Mae Luan

Th Satun

2

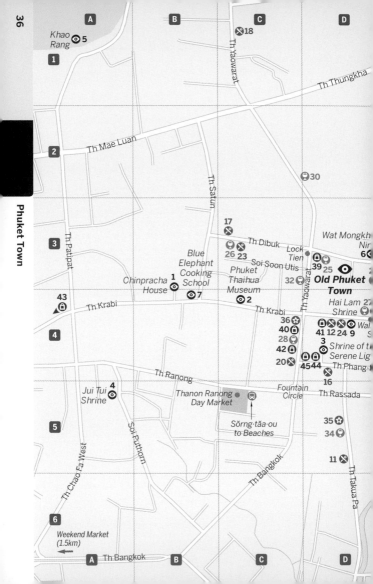30

Th Dibuk

17
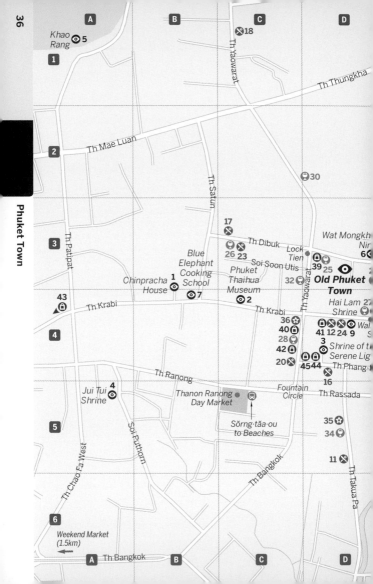

26 23

Blue
Elephant
Cooking
School

Soi Soon Utis

Lock
Tien

39 25

Wat Mongkh
Nir

6

3

Chinpracha
House

1

Phuket
Thaihua
Museum

7

2

32

Old Phuket
Town

Hai Lam 27
Shrine

Th Patipat

Th Krabi

Th Krabi

36
40

28
42

3

41 12 24 9

Wai
S

Shrine of t
Serene Lig

20

45 44

Th Phang-

4

Th Ranong

Jui Tui
Shrine

4

Thanon Ranong
Day Market

Fountain
Circle

16

Th Rassada

5

Sörng·tǎa·ou
to Beaches

35
34

Th Chao Fa West

Soi Puthorn

11

Th Bangkok

Th Takua Pa

6

Weekend Market
(1.5km)

A Th Bangkok **B** **C** **D**

43

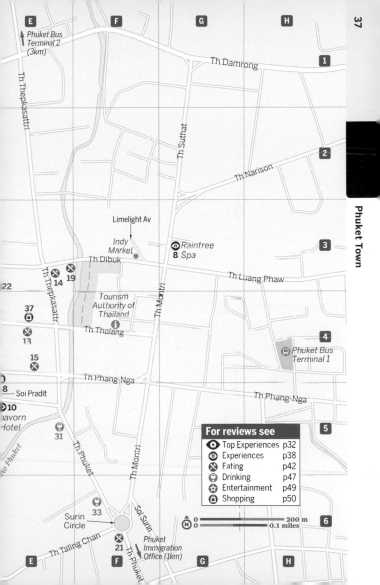

E **F** **G** **H**

1

↑ Phuket Bus
Terminal 2
(3km)

Th Damrong

Th Thepkasattri

Th Suthat

2

Th Narison

Limelight Av

Indy
Market

⊚ Raintree
8 Spa

3

Th Dibuk

Th Luang Phaw

⊗ ⊗
14 **19**

22

Th Thepkasattri

Tourism
Authority of
Thailand ℹ

Th Montri

37
🔒

Th Thalang

4

⊗
13

📍 Phuket Bus
Terminal 1

15
⊗

Th Phang-Nga

Soi Pradit

Th Phang-Nga

8

10

navorn
Hotel

🚌
31

5

Th Phuket

Th Montri

For reviews see
⊙ Top Experiences   p32
⊚ Experiences   p38
⊗ Eating   p42
🍺 Drinking   p47
⭐ Entertainment   p49
🔒 Shopping   p50

Surin
Circle

🚌
33

Soi Surin

Ⓝ 0 _____ 200 m
0 _____ 0.1 miles

6

Th Taling Chan

⊗
21

Th Phuket

Phuket
Immigration
Office (1km)

E **F** **G** **H**

Experiences

Chinpracha House MUSEUM

1 MAP P36, B3

Built in 1903 on tin-mining riches, this beautifully preserved Sino-Portuguese mansion should make any antique- or architecture-lover's list. Others might find the four-poster steel beds done up in Victorian lace a bit gaudy. But the historical details of the atrium foyer – with its arch-framed koi pond, fresh-hibiscus bowls, gorgeous Italian ceramic tiles and vintage black-and-white family portraits – make visits incredibly rewarding. It's still lived in by the sixth-generation descendants of original owner Phra

Fun for the Family

The well-organised, professionally operated adventure space **Hanuman World** (062 979 5533; www.hanumanworld-phuket.com; 105 Mu 4, Th Chao Fa; 1-/2-/3-hr zipline incl sky walk 1990/2300/3190B; 8am-5pm) is sensitively built into the jungle 5km southwest of Phuket Town. Ziplines (seven, 16 or 30 platforms) sweep through a tropical canopy of rambutan and durian trees. For those who'd rather not brave it, there's a skywalk (690B) plus a stylish Thai-international restaurant (110B to 500B) topped by a cocoon-like roof-terrace cocktail bar.

Pitak Chinpracha. (บ้านชินประชา; Baan Chinpracha; 076 211281, 076 211167; 98 Th Krabi; 200B; 9am-4.30pm Mon-Sat)

Phuket Thaihua Museum MUSEUM

2 MAP P36, C4

Founded in 1934 and formerly a Chinese-language school, this flashy museum is filled with photos, videos and English-language exhibits on Phuket's history, from the Chinese migration (many influential Phuketian families are of Chinese origin), the tin-mining era and the Vegetarian Festival (p44) to local cuisine, fashion and literature. The building itself is a stunning combination of Chinese and European architectural styles, including art deco and Palladianism with a Chinese gable roof and stucco, plus a British-iron gate. (พิพิธภัณฑ์ภูเก็ตไทย หัว; 076 211224; 28 Th Krabi; 200B; 9am-5pm)

Shrine of the Serene Light SHRINE

3 MAP P36, D4

A handful of Chinese temples pump colour into Phuket Town, but this restored shrine, tucked away up a 50m alley now adorned with modern murals, is particularly atmospheric, with its Taoist etchings on the walls and the vaulted ceiling stained from incense plumes. The altar is always fresh with flowers and burning candles, and the surrounding Sino-Portuguese buildings have been beautifully repainted. The shrine is said to have been built by a local family in 1889. (ศาลเจ้าแสงธรรม, Saan Jao Sang Tham; Th Phang-Nga; admission free; ⏱8.30am-noon & 1.30-5.30pm)

Jui Tui Shrine

TAOIST SHRINE

4 ⊙ MAP P36, A5

One of the island's most important Chinese shrines, this red-washed, elevated complex is dedicated to Tean Hu Huan Soy, god of performers and dancers. It's also the major base for serious (read: violently pierced) participants during Phuket's Vegetarian Festival (p44). Originally located on Soi Romanee, the shrine dates back to 1911 and relocated to its current position after a fire; today it houses a 21st-century firecracker tower.

Yellow-and-red-signed vegetarian restaurants line Th Ranong nearby. (ศาลเจ้าจุ้ยตุ่ยเต้าโบ้เก้ง; Soi Puthorn; admission free; ⏱8am-8.30pm)

Khao Rang

VIEWPOINT

5 ⊙ MAP P36, A1

For a bird's-eye view of the city, climb (or drive) up Khao Rang, 2.5km northwest of Phuket Town centre. An overhanging viewing platform opens up 270-degree panoramas across Phuket Town to Chalong Bay, Laem Phanwa and Big Buddha. It's at its most peaceful during the week. There are a few restaurants and cafes up here, and **Wat Khao Rang** is worth a look along the way. It's about an hour's walk (but don't try it at night). (เขารัง, Phuket Hill; P)

Jui Tui Shrine

Phuket Food Tours

A Bangkok-born food-tour specialist runs energetic, insightful half-day gastronomic jaunts around Phuket Town (www.phuketfoodtours.com; tour per person 2300-3000B; ☉tour 8am & 4pm), uncovering such unique Phuketian delicacies as Thai dim sum, southern-style *roti* and and *mǒo hong*. On the dedicated Peranakan-cooking and night-food trails, knowledgeable local guides weave together Phuket's history and culinary traditions. Rates include hotel transfers. Book ahead.

Wat Mongkhon Nimit

BUDDHIST TEMPLE

6 ◉ MAP P36, D3

Just beyond the northern end of beautiful Soi Romanee, Phuket Town's 85-year-old working main Buddhist temple is one of the island's four most revered, with a banyan tree in its grounds, an impressive *chedi* and a golden seated Buddha. (วัดมงคลนิมิตร; Th Dibuk; admission free; ☉daylight hours)

Blue Elephant Cooking School

COOKING

7 ◉ MAP P36, B4

Master the intricate art of royal Thai cooking in a stunningly restored Sino-Portuguese mansion, with half-day (morning or afternoon) group classes. Morning sessions

visit the market, while afternoon lessons include a dessert section. Book ahead. (☎076 354355; www.blueelephant.com; 96 Th Krabi; half-day class 3296B; ☉9.30am-4.30pm)

Raintree Spa

SPA

8 ◉ MAP P36, G3

Amid tranquil tropical grounds, Raintree is a step up in price, quality and atmosphere from Phuket Town's storefront spas. Skilled therapists don't just go through the motions here. Get silky-smooth with an aloe-cucumber body wrap or a 'fruit salad' scrub (pineapple, papaya, mango), or keep it classic with an ever-reliable Thai massage. (☎081 892 1001; www.theraintreespa.com; Sino House, 1 Th Montri; massage or treatment 500-1500B; ☉10am-9.30pm)

Hai Lam Shrine

SHRINE

9 ◉ MAP P36, D4

A crimson-coloured Sino-Portuguese facade with bright-yellow flourishes, at the heart of old Phuket Town, gives way to this quiet Chinese shrine. (ศาลเจ้าไหหลำ, Shui Wei Sheng Niang Shrine; 18 Th Thalang; ☉hours vary)

Thavorn Hotel

HISTORIC BUILDING

10 ◉ MAP P36, E5

Opened in 1961 by the tin-mining Chinese-Thai Thavorn Wong Wongse family, the Thavorn was Phuket's original five-star. It's one of the oldest hotels around still operating. Although the facade is

Phuket's History

Phuket's history reads like a Robert Louis Stevenson adventure novel. It features, among other characters, jungle-dwelling indigenous people, savvy Indian and European merchants, (supposedly) marauding sea nomads, immigrant Chinese tin miners, and war heroines who helped save Thailand from Burma's imperial ambition.

Indian merchants founded Phuket Town in the 1st century BC. Greek geographer Ptolemy, who visited in the 3rd century AD, dubbed it 'Jang Si Lang', which later morphed into 'Junk Ceylon'. Among Phuket's original local inhabitants were now-extinct ancient tribes similar to Malaysia's surviving Semang tribes. Meanwhile, sea nomads of Malay descent, known today as *chao lair* (also spelt *chao leh*), populated Phuket's coastal areas; they sailed from cove to cove in hardy houseboats that could weather the roughest seas, living off shellfish and turtle soup, collecting pearls and staying until each beach's resources were depleted.

In the 16th century, the first Europeans descended on Phuket, with Dutch, Portuguese, then French and then British traders arriving for the tin industry. Thousands of Chinese labourers arrived for the tin-mining boom in the latter half of the 19th century. They brought their culinary and spiritual traditions with them and, when they intermarried with local citizens, Phuket's Baba culture was born. In the late 19th and early 20th centuries, the Baba people built up Phuket Town, constructing enormous homes blending Portuguese and Chinese styles, with high ceilings and thick walls to keep them cool. These impressive Sino-Portuguese buildings – many of them now colourfully restored – are Phuket Town's main attractions.

Beach lovers began arriving en masse in the 1970s, transforming Phuket into one of the world's premier beach resorts. Tourism remained strong until the devastating 2004 Boxing Day tsunami, which killed 250 people on Phuket and almost 5400 across Thailand; some estimates have it much higher. Kamala, on the west coast, was particularly badly hit. It was a dark moment in Phuket's history, but Phuketians have bounced back. Today development continues at an increasingly and alarmingly unsustainable rate.

unimpressive, the wood-panelled, memorabilia-packed interior is an instant throwback to earlier times. A grand wooden staircase leads off the wide lobby, which hosts a dusty museum full of tin toys, musical instruments, old movie projectors, historical photos and decades-old

Sampling Local Cuisine

Communal tables cluster under whirring fans at fast-and-furious food court **Lock Tien** (Map p36, D3; cnr Th Dibuk & Th Yaowarat; meals 35-100B; ☺9am-5pm), which works up a vast, tempting range of classic Phuket Town dishes. Sample *popiah sod hokkien* (Fujianese fresh spring rolls, stuffed with prawns or veggies), spicy-sour Hokkien-noodle soup, *lobha* (pork cheek and offal) and more, at down-to-earth prices.

newspaper clippings. (โรงแรมถาวร; www.thavornhotel.com; 74 Th Rassada; museum 50B; ☺museum 7am-5pm)

Eating

Suay   THAI, FUSION $$$

11 🍴 MAP P36, D5

Fabulous fusion and fine wines, courtesy of top Phuket chef-owner Noi Tammasak, are the draw at this converted house just south of the Old Town. Spicy eggplant salads, sweet-basil Shanghai noodles, braised-beef-cheek massaman and grilled lemongrass lamb chops with papaya salsa are just some of the highlights. A new cocktail bar and Thai-tapas menu were in the works at research time. (📞087 888 6990; www.suayrestaurant.com; 50/2 Th Takua Pa; mains 400-1000B; ☺5-11pm)

Kopitiam by Wilai   THAI $

12 🍴 MAP P36, D4

Family-owned Kopitiam serves fabulous Phuket soul food in an atmospheric old shophouse: Phuketian *pàt tai* with a kick, *chai chae* (chilli-dressed noodle salad) and fantastic *mee sua* (noodles sautéed with egg, greens, prawns, sea bass and squid). Wash it all down with fresh chrysanthemum or passion-fruit juice. There are two branches (one air-con), either side of the Oldest Herbs Shop (p50). (📞083 606 9776; www.face book.com/kopitiambywilai; 14 & 18 Th Thalang; mains 95-180B; ☺11am-5pm & 6.30-9pm Mon-Sat; 🛜♿)

Abdul's Roti Shop   BREAKFAST $

13 🍴 MAP P36, E4

Don't miss the chance to try Abdul's legendary, delicious *roti*. At 75 years plus, Abdul has been cooking flaky *roti* at the front of his shop for years. Whether you're for sweet or savoury, this place has it covered, with *roti* served sticky with banana or condensed milk, topped with a fried egg, or plain with spicy chicken, beef or fish massaman. (Th Thalang; *roti* 30-40B; ☺7am-4pm Mon-Sat, to 1pm Sun)

One Chun   THAI $$

14 🍴 MAP P36, E3

One Chun is a sister restaurant to well-established Raya (p45), only the dishes here are cheaper and that's why Phuketians and visiting Thais crowd it out. It boasts superb seafood – the coconut-milk crab curry is arguably Phuket Town's best – but also great roasted-duck red curry and *pàk miang*. The shophouse setting, with 1950s decor, green-painted shutters and patterned-tile floors, fuels the atmosphere. (📞076 355909; 48/1 Th Thepkasattri; mains 100-370B; ⏲10am-10pm; 🛜)

Surf & Turf by Soul Kitchen   FUSION $$

15 ❌ MAP P36, E4

Filled with hand-drawn murals, this relaxed, stylish Thai-German-owned restaurant scores with its elegant twists on European-Thai fusion food, such as homemade sweet-potato ravioli dressed in yellow-curry sauce and thinly sliced Australian beef with prawn tempura. Though not huge, dishes are smartly presented and full of exciting flavours. There's a small but proper wine list, plus daily specials. (📞089 104 7432; www.facebook.com/surfandturf.soulkitchen; 115 Th Phang-Nga; mains 240-420B; ⏲6-10.30pm Mon-Sat; 🛜)

Tu Kab Khao   THAI $$

16 ❌ MAP P36, D4

Red lanterns cascade down this inviting 130-year-old Sino-Portuguese building, now reimagined as a packed-out restaurant devoted to Phuketian cooking. With varnished-concrete floors, sofa chairs and a wall made entirely of mirrors, it brings old-world glamour to sampling local specialities and is a particular hit

Lock Tien

Vegetarian Festival

Deafening popping sounds fill the streets, the air is thick with grey-brown smoke and people traipse along blocked-off city roads, their cheeks pierced with skewers and knives or lamps and tree branches. Some have blood streaming down their fronts or open lashes across their backs. Welcome to the **Vegetarian Festival** (⊙late Sep-Oct), one of Phuket's most important celebrations, centred on Phuket Town.

The festival, which takes place during the first nine days of the ninth lunar month of the Chinese calendar, celebrates the beginning of 'Taoist Lent', when devout Chinese abstain from meat, dairy and alcohol. Most obvious to outsiders are the fast-paced daily processions winding through town with floats of ornately dressed children and gà·teu·i (also spelt kàthoey; Thai transgender and cross dressers), armies of flag-bearing, colour-coordinated young people and men and women engaged in outrageous acts of self-mutilation.

Those participating as mediums bring the nine emperor gods of Taoism to earth by entering a trance state, piercing their cheeks with a variety of objects, sawing their tongues or flagellating themselves with spiky metal balls. The temporarily possessed mediums stop at shopfront altars to pick up offered fruit and tea and bless the house. Frenzied, surreal and overwhelming barely describe it.

Phuket Town's festival focuses on five Chinese temples. **Jui Tui Shrine** (p39), off Th Ranong, is the most important, followed by **Bang Niew** (ศาลเจ้าบางเหนียว; Th Phuket; admission free; ⊙8.30am-10pm) and **Sui Boon Tong** (ศาลเจ้าซุ่ยบุ่นต๊อง; Soi Lorong; admission free; ⊙daylight hours) shrines. There are also events in nearby Kathu (where the festival originated) and Ban Tha Reua. If you stop by any procession's starting point around 6am, you may spot a surprisingly professional, latex-glove-clad crew piercing the devotees' cheeks (not for the faint-hearted). Other ceremonies include firewalking and knife-ladder climbing. Beyond the headlining gore, cheap vegetarian food stalls line the side streets.

There is no record of these acts of devotion associated with Taoist Lent in China. Local Thai-Chinese claim the festival was started in 1825 in Kathu, by a theatre troupe from China that performed a nine-day penance after becoming seriously ill for failing to propitiate the nine emperor gods.

Phuket's **Tourism Authority of Thailand** (Map p37, F4; TAT; ☑076 211036; www.tourismthailand.org/Phuket; 191 Th Thalang; ⊙8.30am-4.30pm) prints festival schedules.

with weekending Bangkokians. Signature dishes – *mŏo hong*, crab-meat curry – are based on the owner's mother's recipes. (☏076 608888; www.facebook.com/ ukabkhao; 8 Th Phang-Nga; mains 160-290B; ⏲11.30am-midnight; 🛜)

Tantitium
THAI $$

17 ❌ MAP P36, C3

A chic revamp has transformed this 1919 Sino-Portuguese building into a fabulous multi-use space strung around a leafy courtyard. Book in for excellent, authentic Phuketian food in a stylish setting – *mŏo hong*, crab-meat curries and ginger-flower fish curries are favourites. The bar mixes brilliant, original artisan cocktails (try the Six Sense; 280B); upstairs, the palm-patterned spa does Thai massages (250B). (☏080 658 5204; www.facebook.com/tantitium; 82-84 Th Dibuk; mains 180-500B; ⏲bar & restaurant 2pm-1am Mon, Tue, Thu & Fri, from noon Sat & Sun, spa 2-10pm Thu-Tue, all closed Wed)

Blue Elephant
THAI $$$

Royal Thai cuisine in royal Thai surroundings. In the beautifully restored, mustard-yellow Phra Pitak Chinpracha Mansion overlooking manicured lawns (see 7 ⊙ Map p36, B4), Blue Elephant is elegant in every way, from the brass cutlery and ornately carved doors to the chequered floors, stellar service and superbly presented dishes. Choose a tasting menu (Peranakan, Thai or chef-chosen) or go à la carte: it's all exquisite. (☏076 354355; www.

blueelephant.com; 96 Th Krabi; mains 350-1000B, tasting menus 1600-2400B; ⏲11.30am-2.30pm & 6.30-10pm; P 🛜 ✏)

Ratcharod Dim Sum
BREAKFAST $

18 ❌ MAP P36, C1

Rooted in the island's Chinese heritage, Thai-style dim sum is a busy affair for Phuketians, and concrete-walled Ratcharod is a Phuket Town favourite. Steaming bamboo pots of super-fresh pork-, shrimp-, crab- and chicken-filled dumplings arrive at terrace tables, to be enjoyed with pour-your-own pandan tea. It's 1km north of central Phuket Town; look for the teapot logo. (☏080 263 4664; www.facebook.com/ babadimsum; 160/5 Th Yaowarat; dim sum 20-80B; ⏲6am-noon)

Raya
THAI $$

19 ❌ MAP P36, E3

Unrenovated, unpretentious and unbelievably good, charming Raya has been serving southern-Thai fare for around 20 years. This two-storey Sino-Portuguese institution keeps things authentic and old-worldly with its jade-hued wood doors, original mosaic floors, gramophone, stained glass and shuttered windows. Standout house dishes include Phuketian *mŏo hong* and creamy crab-meat curry with coconut milk and rice noodles. (☏076 218155; rayarestaurant@gmail. com; 48/1 Th Dibuk; mains 180-650B; ⏲10am-10pm; P)

Gallery Cafe
CAFE $$

20 🍴 MAP P36, C4

Settle in on cushioned booths at this popular arty cafe, surrounded by floors of varnished concrete and yellow walls covered in bright art. The menu is full of hearty international and Thai goodies: all-day breakfasts, pastas, salads, sandwiches, smoothies, homemade veggie burgers. We're still dreaming about the brilliant breakfast bagels and zingy passion fruit, lemongrass and ginger juices. (📞083 105 4715; www.facebook.com/GalleryCafeByPinky; 19 Th Yaowarat; meals 140-350B; ⏰8am-5pm; 🛜🍴)

Mee Ton Poe
NOODLES $

21 🍴 MAP P36, F6

Right on Phuket Town's Clock Tower Circle, among wooden tables and red-plastic stools, third-generation Mee Ton Poe has been pulling in Phuketians since 1946 with its superb noodle dishes, including mèe nam tom poe (Hokkien-noodle soup) and the signature mèe pad hokkien (fried yellow noodles with pork, shrimp, fish balls and veg in a broth). (Th Phuket; meals 50-80B; ⏰8am-8pm; 🛜)

Torry's Ice Cream Boutique
ICE CREAM $$

22 🍴 MAP P36, E3

Phuketians, expats and tourists alike pack into this very popular cafe-style parlour on Phuket Town's most photogenic street for gourmet ice cream, sorbets and Phuket-style desserts. It's a swish setting in a smart, pastel-pink conversion of an old shophouse. Also does coffee, tea and juices. The carrot-and-passion-fruit sorbet is a delight. (📞076 510888; www.torrysicecream.com; Soi Romanee; ice creams & desserts 60-200B; ⏰11am-6pm Tue-Thu, to 9.30pm Fri-Sun)

Charm
THAI $$

23 🍴 MAP P36, C3

Beautifully home-cooked wok-fried mushrooms, coconut-laced vegetable curry, crab-meat curry and spicy roast-coconut salads accompany signature plates of deep-fried garlic fish and mǒo hong at this (yes) utterly charming 'dining gallery' within an exquisitely tiled Sino-Portuguese home. It's a quiet, intimate setting, which means service is attentive and personal. (📞076 530199; www.facebook.com/CharmDeebukPhuket; 93 Th Dibuk; mains 140-450B; ⏰11am-10pm Thu-Tue; 🛜)

China Inn
INTERNATIONAL, THAI $$

24 🍴 MAP P36, D4

The organic movement meets Phuketian cuisine at this restored turn-of-the-20th-century shophouse with beautiful detailing and a hibiscus-dotted courtyard garden. It serves red crab curry, chicken massaman, spicy seafood salads, Hokkien noodles, homemade honey and fresh mint tea, and fruit smoothies. Service and opening hours can be erratic. (📞076 356239; www.facebook.com/chinainnphuket; 20

Th Thalang; mains 95-350B; ⊙9am-5pm Tue-Sun, hours vary; 🐾)

Drinking

Dibuk House COCKTAIL BAR

25 🚇 MAP P36, D3

The tiled floors and flickering candles of a restyled Sino-Portuguese shophouse mark out Phuket Town's most talked-about cocktail bar. Upping the ante for the local artisan-cocktail scene, it's a sultry, moody place: waistcoat-clad mixologists artfully prepare potent, avant-garde cocktails (250B to 350B) at the mirror-backed bar. The delicate Wynn de Fleur stars gin-infused red-berry tea with aloe, lemon and jasmine. (📞086 796 4646; www.facebook.com/dibukhouse; 39/2 Th Dibuk; ⊙7pm-2am)

Shelter Coffee CAFE

26 🚇 MAP P36, C3

Some of Phuket's finest coffee (55B to 150B) is crafted at experimental, national-award-winning Shelter, whose signature caffeine concoction is a 72-hour cold brew. All the classics are artfully presented, with Aeropress and bean-of-the-day options, and there are Thai herbal teas, soul-soothing hot chocolates, and all-day breakfasts and Thai dishes (90B to 160B). Out the back lies a tucked-away garden. (www.facebook.com/thesheltercoffeephuket; 97 Th Dibuk; ⊙8.30am-6pm Thu-Tue; 🛜)

Bookhemian CAFE

27 🚇 MAP P36, D4

Every town should have a coffee house this cool, with a

China Inn

brick-and-concrete split-level design that makes it both cafe and art exhibition space. Used books (for sale) line the front room, bicycles hang from the wall and a Gabriel García Márquez novel is set into the door handle. Gourmet coffee (50B to 90B), juices, cakes, all-day breakfasts (120B to 150B). (☎098 090 0657; 61 Th Thalang; ⊗9am-7pm Mon-Fri, to 8.30pm Sat & Sun; 🛜)

Club No 43
COCKTAIL BAR

28 🗺 MAP P36, C4

Hendrick's bottles filled with red roses and an open-red-brick bar lined with antiques set the creative tone at this experimental crafted-cocktails lounge. Thai herbs infuse such liquid mixes (300B to 380B) as the signature *dôm yam*-inspired, spiced-vodka-based 43 Old Town, served in a teapot. (☎099 305 6333; www.facebook.com/pg/CLUB-NO43-1495032174131850; 43 Th Yaowarat; ⊗6pm-late; 🛜)

DouBrew
COFFEE

29 🗺 MAP P36, D3

Admire Soi Romanee over an expertly crafted nitro cold brew or Aeropress latte from the leafy terrace of fashionable, forward-thinking, friendly cafe DouBrew, set in the mismatched-furniture lobby of the RomManee boutique guesthouse (p145) – a gorgeous old Sino-Portuguese building revamped with deep-aqua walls and concrete floors. Beans are sourced from across Thailand (coffees 50B

to 120B). (www.facebook.com/DouBrewCoffee; Soi Romanee; ⊗8am-7pm Mon-Sat, to 9pm Sun)

Timber Hut
CLUB

30 🗺 MAP P36, D2

Locals, expats and visitors have been packing out this two-floor pub-club nightly for 28 years, downing beers and whisky while swaying to live bands that swing from hard rock to pure pop to hip-hop. No cover charge. (118/1 Th Yaowarat; ⊗6pm-2am)

Quip Sky Bar
ROOFTOP BAR

31 🗺 MAP P36, E5

On the 5th floor of a minimalist boutique hotel with a vintage car in reception, Phuket Town's first rooftop bar sprawls across a breezy raised deck where net 'chairs' extend over a shallow wraparound pool with decorative, Insta-hit blow-up flamingos. You're here for fantastic views across the city to Khao Rang, rather than the cocktails (130B). (☎076 355052; www.quipphuket.com; 54 Th Phuket; ⊗5pm-midnight; 🛜)

Prohibition
COCKTAIL BAR

32 🗺 MAP P36, C3

Plastered with the handprints of former guests, this casual, expat-owned speakeasy-style bar swings it back to the 1920s with its Prohibition-inspired cocktails (220B to 270B), Chalong Bay Rum cinnamon mojitos and fresh-fruit martinis, and a 'secret' room behind a bookshelf door. (☎093 565 6542;

www.prohibitionphuket.com; 87 Th Yaowarat; ⏰5pm-midnight Tue-Sun)

Cue Bar

SPORTS BAR

33 MAP P36, F6

DJ sets, live bands, pool tables and big screens mingle at this lively, laid-back, forever-popular sports bar that makes a great place to meet Phuketians, local expats and fellow travellers over icy Changs (80B) and mean mojitos (140B). (www.facebook.com/CueBarPhuket; Th Phuket; ⏰4pm-late)

Ka Jok See

CLUB, BAR

34 MAP P36, D5

Dripping with Old Phuket charm and the owner's fabulous trinket collection, this intimate, century-old house has two identities: half glamorous restaurant, half crazy party venue. There's good Thai food (buffet 3000B per person), but once the tables are cleared it becomes a bohemian madhouse with top-notch music and – if you're lucky – extravagant cabaret. Book a month or two ahead. (📞076 217903, 095 428 0493; www.facebook.com/kajoksee; 26 Th Takua Pa; ⏰8pm-1am Nov-Apr, reduced hours May-Oct)

Entertainment

Bebop

LIVE MUSIC

35 ⭐ MAP P36, D5

Under the watch of one of the island's favourite musicians, Boy Navio, red-walled Bebop is the place in town for quality live jazz, and gets busy with Phuketians and local expats for its nightly 9.30pm

Central Festival (p51)

performances. (www.facebook.com/
Bebop-Live-Music-Bar-Restaurant-
714269582045888; Th Takua Pa;
🕑2pm-midnight; 📶)

Rockin' Angels
LIVE MUSIC

36 ⭐ MAP P36, C4

An intimate Old Town bar rammed
with biker paraphernalia and
framed LPs. It gets loud when Pat-
rick, the Singaporean-born owner,
jams with his house blues band
from around 9.30pm most nights.
Beers are cold and you'll be surrounded by a good mix of Thais and
local expats. (📞089 654 9654; www.
facebook.com/RockinAngelsCafe; 55 Th
Yaowarat; 🕑6pm-1am Tue-Sun)

Shopping

Ranida
ANTIQUES, FASHION

37 🔒 MAP P36, E4

An elegant antiques gallery and
boutique featuring antiquated Buddha statues and sculptures, organic
textiles, and ambitious, exquisite
high-fashion women's clothing
inspired by vintage Thai garments
and fabrics. (119 Th Thalang; 🕑10am-
8pm Mon-Sat)

Drawing Room
ART

38 🔒 MAP P36, E4

With a street-art vibe reminiscent
of pre-boom Brooklyn or East
London, this wide-open cooperative
is by far the standout gallery in a
town full of them. Original canvases
might be comical pen-and-ink
cartoons or vibrantly abstract,

while techniques range from graffiti
to batik and wood-carving. Metallic
furniture, bicycles and motorbikes
line concrete floors, and house
music thumps at low levels. (www.
facebook.com/DrawingRoomPhuket; 56
Th Phang-Nga; 🕑9.30am-6pm)

Pink Flamingo
FASHION & ACCESSORIES

39 🔒 MAP P36, D3

In a chicly restored old building
with arches over the front door,
this self-styled 'tropical concept
store' is all about floaty fabrics,
bold colours and embroidered
handmade dresses, kaftans
and accessories from Bali. The
upstairs bar-restaurant serves
tapas, salads and pastas (105B to
345B) between gorgeous hand-
painted flamingo-mural walls. On
Instagram @pinkflamingophuket.
(39/12 Th Yaowarat; 🕑10am-8pm)

Ban Boran Textiles
TEXTILES

40 🔒 MAP P36, C4

Shelves at this hole-in-the-wall fashion shop are stocked with quality
silk scarves, Myanmar lacquerware,
sarongs, linen shirts and cotton
textiles from Chiang Mai, and fabrics sourced from Southeast Asia's
tribal communities. (51 Th Yaowarat;
🕑10.30am-6.30pm Mon-Sat)

Oldest Herbs Shop
HEALTH & WELLNESS

41 🔒 MAP P36, D4

You can't miss the wafting aromas
of Phuket's oldest herbs shop as

you stroll along Th Thalang. Stop here to stock up on Chinese herbal remedies or to simply watch portions of herbs being weighed on antique scales and mixed together ready for sale at this century-old, third-generation family business. (Th Thalang; ⊙8am-6pm)

Art Room Phuket ART

42 🔒 MAP P36, C4

Dip into a split-level world of bold, powerful, locally inspired abstract oil canvases that throw light on contentious hot topics such as urban expansion, sea pollution and water shortages, as well as a few delicate watercolours of Phuket Town. (29 Th Yaowarat; ⊙10am-5pm)

Central Festival SHOPPING CENTRE

43 🔒 MAP P36, A4

On the western fringes of town, Phuket's major shopping centre is an air-conditioned giant crammed with international brands like Zara, Mango, Boots and H&M, plus everything else you could possibly need, from food courts to electronics. It also has a cinema, so it's a good place to spend a rainy day. (www.centralfestivalphuket.com; 74-75 Th Wichitsongkran; ⊙10.30am-10pm)

Wua Art Gallery & Studio ART

44 🔒 MAP P36, D4

A fun and intriguing artist-owned shophouse featuring mythical creatures and abstract portraits in minimalist grey-dominated oils

---

To Market, To Market

A wonderful way to embrace Phuket Town's local flavour is by getting lost in its markets. The **Weekend Market** (Map p36, A1; Naka Market; off Th Chao Fa West; ⊙4-10pm Sat & Sun) is the biggest of the bunch, but the Sunday-evening **Walking St** (Map p36, D4; Th Thalang; ⊙4-10pm Sun) in the heart of the Old Town is more atmospheric and originally stocked. There's also the **Indy Market** (Map p37, F3; Limelight Ave; mains 30-100B; ⊙4-10.30pm Wed-Fri), loved by local Phuketians, along with, for fresh produce, **Thanon Ranong Day Market** (Map p36, C5; Th Ranong; mains from 35B; ⊙5am-noon).

---

on canvas, with splashes of vibrant colours, crafted by an artist known as 'Mr Zenn' (check out his work on Instagram @mrzenn). (📞096 635 5984; www.wua-artgallery.com; 50 Th Phang-Nga; ⊙9.30am-9.30pm)

Southwind Books BOOKS

45 🔒 MAP P36, D4

Peruse the dusty aisles here for affordable second-hand paperbacks in various languages, including English, French and German. (📞089 724 2136; www.facebook.com/SouthWindBooks; 3-9 Th Phang-Nga; ⊙9am-10pm Mon-Sat)

Worth a Trip 👀
Laem Phanwa

An elongated jungle-cloaked cape jutting into the sea south of Phuket Town, Laem Phanwa (แหลม พันวา) is an all-natural throwback. Some say this is the very last vestige of Phuket as it once was. The biggest bloom of development is near the harbour at the cape's tip. On either side of the harbour, the beaches and coves remain rustic, protected by rocky headlands and mangroves and reached by a leafy, sinuous coastal road.

From Th Ranong in Phuket Town, *sŏrng·tăa·ou* (passenger pick-up trucks) travel southeast to Laem Phanwa from 8am to 5.30pm (30B); the last stop is the Phuket Aquarium.

Taxis to/from Phuket Town cost 400B.

Sunsets & Cocktails

Engulfed by beautiful Andaman and island views and bordered by glittering reflective pools, the elegant, intimate rooftop **Baba Nest lounge-bar** (076 371000; www.babaphuket.com; Sri Panwa, 88 Mu 8, Th Sakdidej; 5-9pm;) is a truly magical spot – and one of the island's (and Thailand's) prime sunset-watching hang-outs, with smartly prepared classic cocktails (500B to 1000B) and Mexican-inspired tapas (350B). Book several weeks ahead; reservations require a 2000B minimum spend.

Spa Time

One of Phuket's top spas, **Cool Spa** (076 371000; www.coolspaphuket.com; Sri Panwa, 88 Mu 8, Th Sakdidej; treatment from 4500B; 10am-9pm) is an elegant wonderland of delicate blue tiling, hillside ocean-view pools, six waterfall treatment rooms, and fruit-infused wraps, facials and scrubs. And there's the dreamy setting on the southernmost tip of Laem Phanwa. Treatments mix Thai, Indian, Balinese and Swedish techniques; signature Thai massages are done in a classic style on a floor mattress.

Phuket Aquarium

Get a glimpse of Thailand's wondrous underwater world at Phuket's popular **aquarium** (pictured left; สถานแสดงพันธุ์สัตว์น้ำภูเก็ต; 076 391406; www.phuketaquarium.org; 51 Th Sakdidej; adult/child 180/100B; 8.30am-4.30pm;), by the harbour on the tip of Laem Phanwa. It's not the largest collection of marine life, but there are useful English-language displays and captions. Check out the blacktip reef shark, the tiger-striped catfish resembling a marine zebra, the electric eel with a shock of up to 600V, and the 80-million-baht multimedia Aqua Dome, launched in 2018.

★ **Top Tips**

○ Laem Phanwa is where you go to escape the rest of Phuket; don't expect a huge amount of entertainment.

○ If budget allows, book well ahead for drinks at glamorous Baba Nest, one of the island's most exquisite sunset-gazing spots.

○ From outside the Phuket Aquarium, you can charter long-tail boats to offshore islands such as Ko Bon and Coral Island. Prices depend on your bargaining skills.

✕ **Take a Break**

There are seafood restaurants along the harbour waterfront where you can watch the fishing boats bobbing by, or dine at one the excellent restaurants at Sri Panwa resort (p145).

Explore
Hat Patong

Pulling together mass tourism's most discouraging traits, party-hard Patong (ป่าตอง) is a free-for-all: a hectic jumble of uncontrolled development, neon-lit go-go bars and hard-hustling vendors, all with a decidedly sleazy feel. That said, thousands of holidaymakers still flock to Patong's clubs, restaurants and sweeping white sands each year – in fact, it's the island's most popular beach. It's also the core of Phuket's LGBT+ scene. If you're after a party, Patong is the place.

The Short List

○ **Delicious Dining (p63)** Diving into the Patong food scene.

○ **Club Scene (p67)** Partying until dawn at Phuket's world-famous megaclubs.

○ **Hat Freedom (p60)** Escaping to this silky strand for a hint of where Patong's original popularity stems from.

○ **LGBT+ Phuket (p68)** Drinking, dancing and glittery cabaret at the heart of the island's LGBT+ scene.

○ **Pub Crawl (p56)** Wandering between Patong's most laid-back boozers.

Getting There & Around

🚗 To/from airport 800B.

🚌 Phuket Smart Bus to/from airport (150B, hourly), west coast beaches and Rawai. Local buses (30B) and minivans (50B) to/from Phuket Town's Bus Terminal 1 (7am to 5pm).

Sŏrng·tăa·ou Passenger pick-up trucks to/from Phuket Town (30B, 7.30am to 6pm).

Hat Patong Map on p58

Hat Patong (p62) on Chinese New Year JOEY SANTINI/SHUTTERSTOCK ©

Walking Tour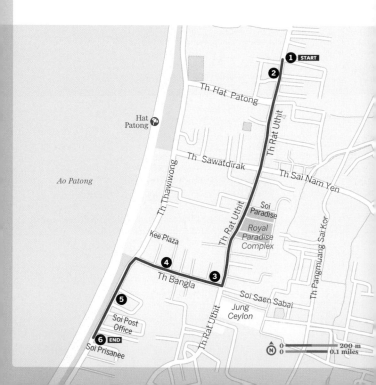

Patong Pub & Grub Crawl

A night out in Patong is obligatory for party lovers on Phuket and inevitably involves a good few laps along Th Bangla. This walk takes in a few of the less, er, sordid spots to fill up on beers, booze and snacks. On the surface the atmosphere is more carnival than carnage, and there are a few harmless bars scattered around.

Walk Facts
Start Nicky's Handlebar
End Molly's Tavern
Length 2km; six hours

❶ Nicky's Handlebar

Kick things off at long-standing biker hangout **Nicky's Handlebar** (☎084 824 7777; www.nickyhandle bars.com; 41 Th Rat Uthit; ☺7am-1am; 🛜), which claims to sizzle up Thailand's spiciest burgers; ask about the exhilarating Harley tours while you're here, too.

❷ Patong Food Park

Amble south along Patong's main street Th Rat Uthit, passing row upon row of seafood restaurants and noodle stalls. Near the intersection with Th Hat Patong, you'll find Patong Food Park, a cheap-food, plastic-chair affair. Always busy, it's ideal for easing into a heavy night, with fresh fish, crab, lobster, satay, roasted pork, steamed chicken and *sôm·dam* (spicy green-papaya salad).

❸ Thanon Bangla

Head south again, then turn right (west) on to **Th Bangla**. For many travellers Th Bangla *is* Patong: go-go bars, ping-pong sex shows and dusk-till-dawn debauchery, with the usual mix of bored-looking gyrating Thai women and red-faced foreign men. For others, it's a one-night experience before a hasty retreat.

❹ Aussie Bar

Push west through the crowds towards Hat Patong. The **Aussie Bar** (www.phuketaussiebar.com; 9/1 Th Bangla; ☺9am-3am; 🛜) is pretty good fun if you've had enough of Th Bangla's street circus; get competitive on the pool tables or catch up on the football, rugby, tennis, cricket etc splashed across huge screens.

❺ Wine Connection

Battle your way past club touts to the western end of Th Bangla. Turn left (south) on Th Thawiwong to reach Bangkok-born **Wine Connection** (☎076 510622; www.wine connection.co.th; 1st fl, Banana Walk, Th Thawiwong; ☺noon-midnight) and enjoy well-priced wines, pastas, pizzas, charcuterie and cheese boards at terrace tables just over the road from the beach.

❻ Phuket's Original Pub

A few steps south along Th Thawiwong, Phuket's oldest pub, **Molly's Tavern** (☎086 911 6194; www.mollysphuket.com; 94/1 Th Thawiwong; ☺10am-2am), is looking refreshed after a makeover and rebrand. Packed with pool tables and sports screens, this cheery Irish-style boozer gets lively with happy hour from 10am to 6pm daily, live music 9.30pm Tuesday to Saturday and solid pub grub.

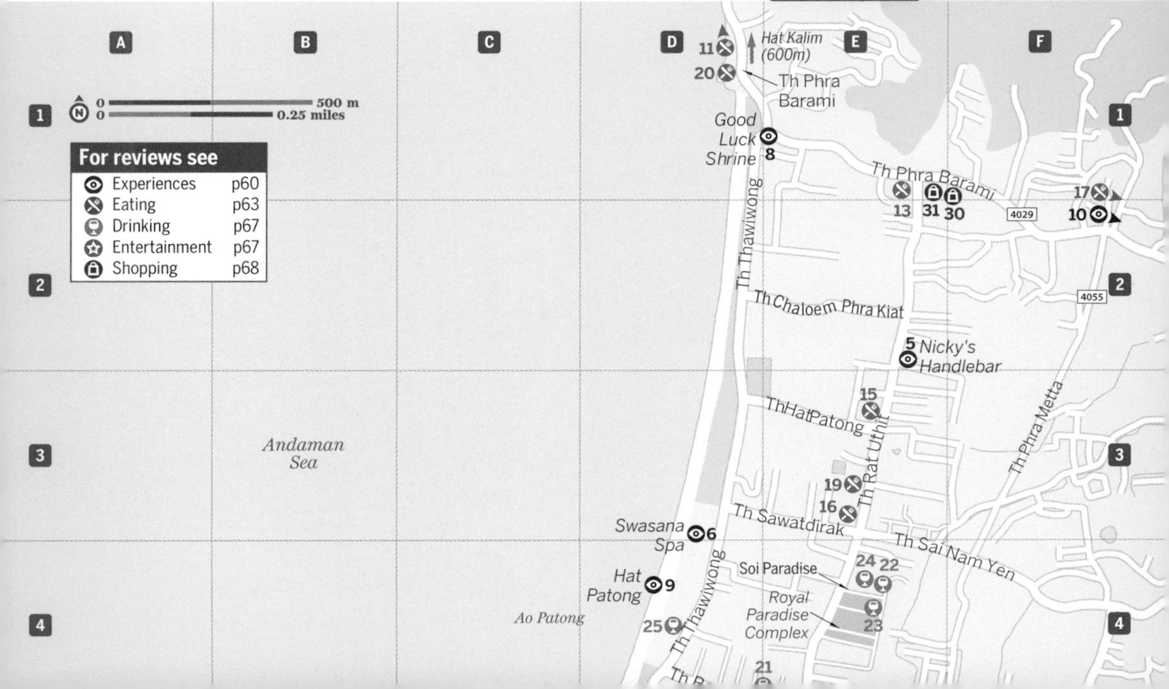

Hat Patong

500 m
0.25 miles

For reviews see
Experiences	p60
Eating	p63
Drinking	p67
Entertainment	p67
Shopping	p68

Andaman Sea

Hat Kalim (600m)

Th Phra Barami

4029

Th Phra Barami

Good Luck Shrine 8

Th Thawiwong

Th Chaloem Phra Klat

Th Phra Barami

13 31 30

5 Nicky's Handlebar

17
10

4055

2

Th Phra Metta

Th Rat Uthit

15

19
16

Th Hat Patong

Th Sawatdirak

Swasana Spa 6

Hat Patong 9

Th Sai Nam Yen

24 22

Soi Paradise

Royal Paradise Complex

23

25

21

Th Thawiwong

Ao Patong

11
20

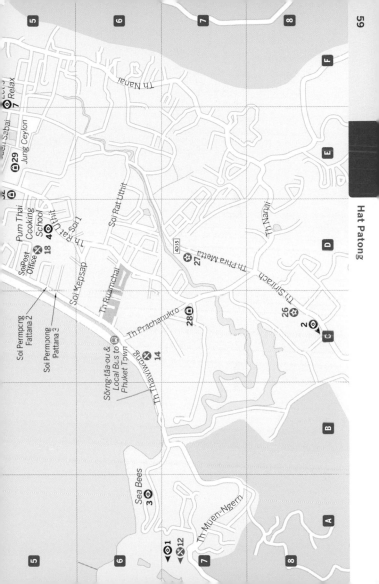

Hat Patong

Th Nanai

Relax 7

Jung Ceylon 29

Pum Thai Cooking School 4

SoiPost Office 18

Soi Rat Uthit

Soi Rat Uthit 1

Soi Kepsap

Soi Permong Pattana 2

Soi Permong Pattana 3

Th Ruamchai

Th Prachanukro

Söng·täa·ou & Local Buses to Phuket Town

Th Thawiwong

14

28

4035

27

26

2

Th Phra Metta

Th Sirirach

Th Nanai

Sea Bees 3

Th Muen-Ngern

1

12

Experiences

Hat Freedom
BEACH

1 MAP P59, A7

If Patong is getting to you, escape to this more peaceful slice of golden sand washed by clear aqua water. It's just 15 minutes or a 1500B (return) long-tail boat ride south around the headland from Hat Patong. You can also get here via a challenging walk from a parking area 900m south of the Avista Hideaway Resort, beyond the southern end of Patong (though the path isn't always open). (ชายหาดเสรีภาพ)

Jet-ski Scams ⚠

If you're hiring a jet ski, especially on Hat Patong, be aware of one of Phuket's biggest scams. There are endless reports of jet-ski owners who, upon your return, claim you've caused damage to the watercraft when in fact it was pre-existing. Things can turn nasty: tourists constantly report extortion attempts, physical threats and intervention by police, often allegedly involved in the scam. To avoid these unpleasant encounters, insist on inspecting the jet ski prior to use, particularly underneath and along the sides, and take photos.

Sea Fun Divers
DIVING

2 MAP P59, C8

Based at Le Méridien, just beyond the southern end of Patong, this is an excellent, professional diving operation, with high standards, impeccable service and enthusiastic, well-versed instructors (though it's a little more expensive than others). Snorkellers can join diving day trips for 2900B. PADI Open Water Diver certification costs 18,400B to 21,400B. (📞081 367 4542; www.seafundivers.com; 29 Soi Karon Nui; 2/3-dive trip 3900/4400B; ⏱9am-6pm)

Sea Bees
DIVING

3 MAP P59, A6

An excellent, efficient, German-managed diving school offering fun dives to Ko Phi-Phi and Ko Raya, Open Water Diver SSI certification (three days, 15,000B) and Similan Islands liveaboards (from 18,900B). Snorkellers are welcome to join dive trips (2400B). Has branches across Phuket, including **Hat Nai Yang** (📞076 327006; www.sea-bees.com; Slate, 116 Mu 1, Hat Nai Yang; 2-dive trip 3500B; ⏱hours vary), and Khao Lak. (📞076 381705; www.sea-bees.com; Amari Phuket, 2 Th Muen-Ngern; 2-dive trip 3800B; ⏱9am-6pm)

Pum Thai Cooking School
COOKING

4 MAP P59, D5

This restaurant/cookery school (with other branches in Thailand, as well as France and the UK) holds daily small-group classes.

Popular, four-hour 'Little Wok' courses (2400B) include a market tour and a take-home cookbook, or pop in for a 30-minute, one-dish session (500B). (☎076 346269; www.pumthaifoodchain.co.th; 204/32 Th Rat Uthit; 3/5hr class 1700/3700B; ⏰classes 11am, 4pm & 6pm)

Nicky's Handlebar ADVENTURE

5 MAP P58, E2

The big-beast bikes here are begging to be taken for a spin, but they aren't for amateurs. Nicky has been leading Harley tours around Phuket and Phang-Nga for over a decade. Two-day itineraries tour Phang Nga and Ranong provinces. There are Harley rentals for independent explorations too (from 4800B). You'll need a big-bike license from home. (☎084 824 7777; www.nickyhandlebars.com; 41 Th Rat Uthit; 1-/2-day tour incl bike hire from 9000/21,000B; ⏰7am-1am)

Swasana Spa SPA

6 MAP P58, D3

This professional four-star spa sits right on the beach, within the **Impiana Resort Patong** (d incl breakfast 7400-23,600B; P ❄ 📶 🏊), towards the slightly quieter northern end of Hat Patong. The best deal is the traditional Thai massage (1500B), though there's a wealth of wraps, scrubs and facials too. You'll be nestled in a glass cube on a cushy floor mat with ocean views. (☎076 340138; www.impiana.com; Impiana Resort Patong, 41 Th Thawiwong; massage or treatment 1500-6900B; ⏰10am-7pm)

Hat Patong (p62)

Tiger Kingdom

Launched in 2013, Phuket's controversial Tiger Kingdom offers hundreds of daily visitors the chance to stroke, feed and pose overenthusiastically with its 'domesticated' tigers, both tiny cubs and full-grown adults.

As with Thailand's other tiger-centric attractions, concerns about animal welfare (not to mention human safety) abound, and there are constant reports about animals being maltreated, confined to small cages and sedated to keep them docile. Like the infamous Tiger Temple in Kanchanaburi, which was raided in 2016 and accused of illegally possessing and trafficking tigers, Tiger Kingdom denies all allegations that its tigers are mistreated.

In 2014, an Australian tourist was seriously mauled while visiting Tiger Kingdom. The tiger in question was 'retired'.

Given the significant animal-welfare issues involved, Lonely Planet does not recommend visiting Tiger Kingdom.

Let's Relax   SPA

7 MAP P59, F5

The hushed atrium, infused with eucalyptus, is perfect for mulling over your relaxation strategy at this prize-winning Thailand-wide spa chain. Will it be foot reflexology, then a floral body scrub? A Thai herbal steam bath before a hot-stone massage and a facial? The all-in, half-day Day Dream package (4000B)? (☏076 366800; www.letsrelaxspa.com; 184/14 Th Pang-muang Sai Kor; massage or treatment 300-4000B; ⊙10am-midnight)

Good Luck Shrine   SHRINE

8 MAP P58, E1

A beautiful, golden Bodhisattva statue in the middle of a traffic circle, adorned with rainbow-coloured ribbons and guarded by carved elephants festooned with flowers, incense and candles. Given the sea backdrop, this is a pleasant spot to connect with the divine or simply make a wish and savour the sound of...passing cars. (ศาลเจ้าโชคดี; cnr Th Thawiwong & Th Phra Barami)

Hat Patong   BEACH

9 MAP P58, D4

It may not be a blissful stretch of untouched paradise, but Patong's ever-popular broad white-sand beach is action-packed, with sunloungers, umbrellas and loads of water activities on offer. (หาดป่าตอง)

Wat Suwan Khiri Wong   BUDDHIST TEMPLE

10 MAP P58, F2

This slightly overgrown yet peaceful compound, just off Th Phra Barami at the northeast end of Patong, is a welcome respite from the chaos outside. Unlike some of Phuket's more tourist-friendly temples, it's home to rambling roosters, dozing dogs and locked temple doors. The elaborately tiered roof of the crematorium is beautiful. (วัดสุวรรณคีรีวงค์; cnr Th Phra Barami & Th Phisit Karani; admission free; ☉daylight hours)

Eating

Acqua ITALIAN, SARDINIAN $$$

 11 ✖ MAP P58, D1

Dine on, say, home-baked focaccia, deliciously creamy buffalo mozzarella and house-made pumpkin-stuffed cappelletti coated in delicate Gorgonzola sauce at Phuket's top Italian restaurant, amid sleek, monochrome decor. From expertly crafted pizza and pasta to sensational seafood blowouts, Sardinian chef Alessandro Frau's cooking is exquisitely executed and supremely sophisticated. Most of the produce is authentic imported Italian, accompanied by 400-plus wines. (☏076 618127; www.acquarestaurantphuket.com; 324/15 Th Phra Barami, Hat Kalim; mains 400-2000B, 8-course tasting menu 2500-3500B; ☉5-11pm mid-Jun–late May; P 🛜 🖥)

Ta Khai THAI $$$

12 ✖ MAP P59, A7

Inspired by traditional fishing-village architecture, with lotus ponds, a glassed-in pavilion and skilled Trang-born chefs, the outstanding, seaside southern-Thai restaurant at the **Rosewood** (villa incl breakfast 24,000-59,600B; P ❄ 🛜 🏊) is a standout in Phuket's fine-dining scene. Fresh *sôm·đam* is pounded at your table; green vegetable

curries, Phuket-style spring rolls, crab-meat yellow curries and Phuketian *mŏo hong* (pepper-and-garlic-braised pork) are beautifully spiced. Signature cocktails use homegrown herbs. (☏076 356888; www.rosewoodhotels.com; Rosewood Phuket, Th Muen-Ngern, Hat Tri-Trang; mains 290-900B, tasting menus 950-2200B; ☉6pm-midnight; P 🛜 🖥)

No 9 2nd Restaurant ASIAN, INTERNATIONAL $$

13 ✖ MAP P58, E1

Deceptively simple, with wooden tables and photo-strewn walls, this is one of the best and busiest restaurants in Patong, thanks to its inventive and delicious mix of Thai, Japanese and Western dishes. It's a rare feat for a kitchen to serve real deal sushi, vegetarian Thai curries and meats such as lamb shank without any dip in quality (☏076 624445; 143 Th Phra Barami; mains 165-800B; ☉11.30am-11.30pm)

Rustic Eatery & Bar MEDITERRANEAN $$$

14 ✖ MAP P59, C6

This stylish, indoor-outdoor restaurant under a canopy of bamboo at the southern end of Patong beach is very popular. It has excellent gourmet pizzas, solid (if pricey) Mediterranean-style mains and charming service. Pick from creative salads, seafood pastas and gourmet burgers, colourfully chalked up on the board, or swing by for tasty breakfasts of pancakes, omelettes and fruit salads.

(☑076 344776; Th Thawiwong; mains 250-850B; ⏱8am-10pm Tue-Sun; 📶)

Chicken Rice Briley
THAI $

15 ❌ MAP P58, E3

This is one of few places in **Patong Food Park** (mains 50-200B; ⏱4.30pm-midnight) to offer sustenance while the sun shines, and it's almost always busy. Steamed chicken breast is served on rice alongside a bowl of chicken broth with crumbled bits of meat; the chilli sauce is fantastic for dipping. The roasted pork on rice and mango sticky rice are popular too. (Th Rat Uthit, mains 50-200B; ⏱6am-9pm)

Georgia Restaurant
GEORGIAN $$

16 ❌ MAP P58, E3

The influx of Russian visitors to Patong has seen a corresponding rise in eateries catering to them. Cosy Georgia is the pick of the bunch, turning out Russian salads and steaming dumplings alongside delicious *khachapuri* (a cheese-filled bread), *ajapsandali* (a rich, vegetarian stew) and classic Eastern European dishes such as *solyanka* (a spicy, sour meat soup in a clay pot). (☑076 390595; www.facebook.com/restaurantgeorgia; 19 Th Sawatdirak; mains 200-400B; ⏱noon-11.30pm Dec-Mar, to 9.30pm Apr-Nov; 📶)

Kaab Gluay
THAI $$

17 ❌ MAP P58, F1

At the north end of town, busy, semi-open-air, roadside Kaab Gluay is a hit for its authentic, affordable Thai food, with switched-on staff to match unpretentious dining under a huge roof with ceiling fans. Expect red-curry prawns, chicken satay, sweet-and-sour fish, deep-fried honeyed chicken, classic noodles and stir-fries, and 30-plus takes on spicy Thai salads. (☑076 346832; 58/3 Th Phra Barami; mains 135-250B; ⏱11am-2am; 📶)

Ella
INTERNATIONAL, BREAKFAST $$

18 ❌ MAP P59, D5

This moulded-concrete, industrial-feel bistro-cafe is a stylish surprise down a slightly scruffy *soi* (lane). Inventive all-day breakfasts mean spicy Rajasthani scrambled eggs, massaman chicken tacos, veg-stuffed omelettes and baguette French toast with caramelised banana. At night, it morphs into a fun bar for cocktails (220B to 300B). (☑076 344253; www.theellagroup.org; 100/19-20 Soi Post Office; mains 150-400B; ⏱7am-midnight; 📶)

Naughty Nuri's in the Forest
RIBS $$

19 ❌ MAP P58, E3

Meat lovers crowd out an enormous, semi-open, multiroom space with swaying rattan lamps at the hugely popular Phuket outpost of this Bali-born, Australian-Indonesian-owned ribs specialist. Make sure you order the signature barbecue spare ribs (1995B), though the spiced suckling pig is also a huge hit, and the Indonesian-international menu tempts with vegetarian nasi goreng and more.

📞061 173 0011; www.facebook.com/
inphuket; 112 Th Rat Uthit; mains 250-
2000B; ⏱noon-midnight)

La Gritta
ITALIAN $$$

A spectacularly positioned, smart
Italian restaurant (see 3 ⊙ Map p59,
6) serving up generous portions of
deliciously creamy pasta, gourmet
pizza and meat and seafood mains
such as Australian beef and fried
lemon-and-wine snapper. It's idyllic
for sunset Chalong Bay Rum mo-
jitos, with comfy booths, gorgeous
beach views and a deck just above
the boulder-strewn shore at the
south end of Hat Patong. (📞076
290967; www.lagritta.com; Amari
Phuket, 2 Th Muen-Ngern; mains 390-
300B; ⏱10.30am-11.30pm; 📶)

Sala Bua
FUSION $$$

Asian-Mediterranean fusion cuisine
in a classy seaside four-star resort
(see 6 ⊙ Map p58, D3) setting. Start with
smoked-salmon Caesar salad or
rock lobster, avocado and roasted
veg salad, then move on to wood-
fired pizzas, seafood-packed spa-
ghetti or jazzed-up fusion curries.
(📞076 340138; www.impiana.com; Im
piana Resort Patong, 41 Th Thawiwong;
mains 250-650B; ⏱11am-11pm)

Baan Rim Pa
THAI $$$

20 🍴 MAP P58, D1

Refined Thai fare is served with a
side order of spectacular views
at this elegant institution hanging
over the rocky far northern end of
Patong beach. Standards are high,
with prices to match, but romance

Hat Patong Eating

Baan Rim Pa

Sex Tourism: The Facts

Thailand has a long and complex relationship with sex tourism. Today it's an industry that most obviously targets foreign tourists – a legacy from the Vietnam War. Despite government crackdowns on corruption since 2014 and assertions from Thailand's tourism body that it opposes sex tourism, it remains very visible. On Phuket, this is especially so in Patong.

Due to international pressure from the UN, prostitution was declared illegal in 1960. Unfortunately, laws against prostitution are often ambiguous, unenforced and, according to Thailand's sex-worker organisation EMPOWER (Education Means Protection of Women Engaged in Recreation), outdated. Furthermore, the unintended consequence of prostitution prohibitions is the lawless working environment it creates for men and women who enter the industry. Sex work becomes the domain of criminal networks often involved in other illicit activities, circumventing laws through bribes, intimidation and violence.

According to a 2014 UNAIDS report, there are around 123,530 sex workers in Thailand. They have no minimum wage; no required holiday, sick leave or break time; no deductions for social security or employer-sponsored health insurance; and no legal redress. Bars set their own punitive rules that fine workers if they don't smile enough, they arrive late, gain weight or don't meet their drinks quota.

UNAIDS' report suggests that at least 40% of Thailand's sex workers are thought to be aged under 18, and of this amount a significant number are boys. According to End Child Prostitution & Trafficking (ECPAT), in 2011 there were up to 60,000 children involved in prostitution in Thailand, though estimates vary wildly. In 1996 Thailand passed a reform law to address the issue of child prostitution. Fines and jail time are assigned to customers, establishment owners and even parents involved in child prostitution (under the old law only prostitutes themselves were culpable). Many countries have extraterritorial legislation that allows nationals to be prosecuted in their own country for such crimes committed in Thailand.

Responsible travellers can report suspicious behaviour on dedicated hotlines (☎1178) or report offenders directly to the relevant embassies, and Thailand is now actively encouraging visitors to do so with country-wide campaigns.

is in the air, with candlelight and piano music aplenty. Reserve ahead. There's another branch nearby on

Hat Kalim. (☎076 340789; www.baanrimpa.com; 223 Th Phra Barami; mains 250-650B; ☺noon-10.30pm)

Drinking

Illuzion

CLUB

21 MAP P58, E4

Still the most popular of Patong's megaclubs, Illuzion is a multilevel mishmash of dance and gymnastics shows, international DJs, reggaeton nights, all-night electronic beats, LED screens and more bars than you could ever count. (www.illuzion phuket.com; 31 Th Bangla; 9pm-late)

Zag Club

GAY, BAR

22 MAP P58, E4

Packed-out Soi Paradise favourite Zag Club hosts fabulous, shimmering LGBT+ cabarets from midnight. In between, everyone drinks and dances to booming chart-toppers. It's usually Patong's busiest gay bar. (www.facebook.com/phuket.zag club; 123/8-9 Royal Paradise Complex; 8pm-4am)

Boat Bar

GAY, BAR

23 MAP P58, E4

Founded by the pioneering LGBT+-bar owner Khun Daeng, Phuket's original gay nightspot puts on sparkling, quality cabaret shows nightly at 11.45pm and 1.30am. (076 341237; www.facebook.com/boatbar; 125/20 Royal Paradise Hotel Complex; 9pm-4am)

My Way

GAY, BAR

24 MAP P58, E4

Popular nightly cabaret shows are staged at this gay-scene original,

Connect Four

Connect Four seems a tame enough pastime when you stroll into the bar on Patong's Th Bangla; you'll play a game or two for a few hundred baht over a few Singhas. But your opponent is a Connect Four mastermind. She will win quickly and easily, every time. Be afraid. Be very afraid. And perhaps avoid Connect Four at all times.

one of Patong's earliest Paradise Complex bars. (125/15-17 Royal Paradise Complex; 8pm-2am)

KUDO Beach Club

LOUNGE

25 MAP P58, D4

Phuket's beach-club scene hits Patong with this buzzing lounge set around a shimmering seafront pool and swim-up bar with chill-out beats and DJ sets. Day beds require a 2000B minimum spend and sunloungers 200B. Friday is pool-party day. It's not as glam as beach clubs further north, but it's a popular spot. (091 842 4303; www.kudophuket.com; Th Thawiwong; 11am-midnight)

Entertainment

Phuket Simon Cabaret

CABARET

26 MAP P59, C8

About 500m south of town, Simon puts on colourful cabarets that

Phuket Pride & LGBT+ Phuket

Although Bangkok and Pattaya host big LGBT+ pride celebrations, **Phuket Pride Week** (www.phuket-pride.org; ⏰Apr) is widely considered to be the best in Thailand, possibly even in Southeast Asia. Dates have changed several times since the festival's inception in 1999 (including a complete hiatus for 2018), but it's usually late April. Revellers, mostly male, descend from all over the world, especially on Patong.

The four-day weekend party takes in a huge beach-volleyball tournament, cruises to nearby islands, beauty contests and the Grand Parade, during which floats, cheering crowds and fabulous sparkly costumes take over Patong's streets. In recent years, the festival has also included fundraising and social-responsibility campaigns to increase awareness of child prostitution, substance abuse and HIV.

At any time of year, you'll find Phuket's LGBT+ pulse in Patong's **Royal Paradise Complex**, the network of streets that links the Royal Paradise Hotel with Th Rat Uthit. It's a predominantly male scene.

Utopia (www.utopia-asia.com) posts lots of Thailand information for LGBT+ travellers and publishes a guidebook to the kingdom. For updates on Phuket's scene, check out Gay Patong (www.gaypatong.com).

are wildly popular with (and now slightly catered towards) tour groups. The 600-seat theatre is grand, the costumes are feather-and-sequin feathery extravaganzas, and the LGBT+ performers are convincing. The house is usually full – book ahead. (✆087 888 6888; www.phuket-simoncabaret.com; 8 Th Sirirach; adult 800-1000B, child 600-800B; ⏰shows 6pm, 7.30pm & 9pm)

Galaxy Boxing Stadium   SPECTATOR SPORT

27 ⭐ MAP P59, D7

A packed line-up of competitive *moo·ay tai* (Thai boxing) bouts featuring Thai and foreign fighters. (www.galaxyboxingstadium.com; Th Phra Metta/Rte 4055; stadium/ringside 1700/2000B; ⏰9pm Tue)

Shopping

Baanboonpitak   ANTIQUES

28 🔒 MAP P59, C7

Hidden in this dusty antiques repository at the southern end of Patong is a vast array of teak sculpture, Buddha images, some excellent bronze work, massive buffalo-skin drums, wood-carved elephants and a lot of high-quality teak furniture. Dig around and you're bound to find something beautiful. The shopkeeper can arrange shipping. (✆081 569 6474; 30 Th Prachanukhro; ⏰10am-11pm, hours vary)

ung Ceylon SHOPPING CENTRE

9 🔒 MAP P59, E5

gleaming shopping centre with
iller air-con and a host of major
rands (Starbucks, Mango, Havai-
nas, the Body Shop) as well as
inema multiplexes and small-scale
nassage parlours. The Sino-Phuket
ving has decent international res-
aurants, while outside, surrounded
y pools and musical fountains,
tands a life-size model of a Chi-
ese junk ship. (www.jungceylon.com;
h Rat Uthit; ⊙11am-10pm)

op Art ART

0 🔒 MAP P58, F1

)ne of several local artist-owned
alleries poised at the north end
f Patong. Expect bright, bold
anvases of classic Thai scenes

(floating markets, coconut drinks,
tigers, elephants, boats bobbing
on the sea) along with some more
abstract pieces. (📞089 197 6778;
www.facebook.com/thenopart; 133 Th
Phra Barami; ⊙8am-10pm)

Art Heart Gallery ART

31 🔒 MAP P58, E1

Vibrant abstract artworks make
this an intriguing pick among the
local artist galleries on this corner.
(cnr Th Rat Uthit & Th Phra Barami;
⊙10am-10pm)

Central Patong SHOPPING CENTRE

32 🔒 MAP P59, E5

This massive, new megamall opposite Jung Ceylon, is slated to open
in 2019. Expect buckets of Thai and
international brands. (Th Rat Uthit)

Phuket Simon Cabaret (p67)

Explore ◈
Hat Karon

Hat Karon (หาดกะรน) is like the love child of Hat Patong and Hat Kata: chilled-out and starry-eyed but still a tad sleazy. With more sand space per capita than Patong or Kata, Karon remains popular with families. The further north you go the more beautiful the broad golden beach gets, culminating at the northernmost edge, beyond Karon Park, where the water is like turquoise glass. Southern Karon blends into more sophisticated Kata.

The Short List

○ **Hat Karon (p73)** Lazing on honey-coloured sands or getting active with a surf session.

○ **Big Buddha Hike (p73)** Clambering up through the lush jungle to the spectacular hilltop Big Buddha.

○ **Spa Time (p73)** Relaxing with tropical-fruit-infused treatments at one of Karon's mellow spas.

Getting There & Around

🚗 Airport (1000B), Phuket Town (550B), Patong (400B).

🚌 Phuket Smart Bus to/from airport (150B hourly), west coast beaches and Rawai. Shared minibus from airport (200B).

Sŏrng·tǎa·ou Passenger pick-up trucks to/from Phuket Town (40B, 7.30am to 6pm).

Hat Karon Map on p72

Hat Karon THAISIGN/SHUTTERSTOCK ©

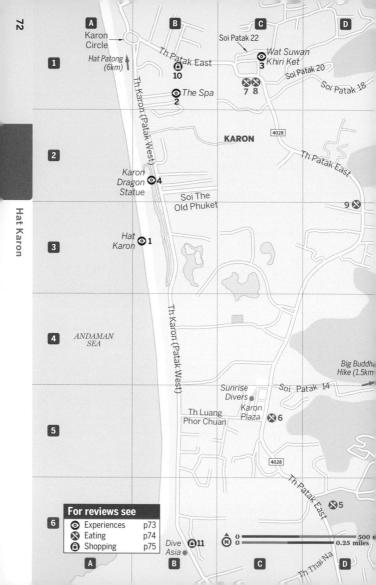

Hat Karon

A Karon Circle

Hat Patong (6km) ↑

Th Patak East

Th Karon (Patak West)

B

Soi Patak 22

☐ 10

◉ The Spa
2

C

◉ Wat Suwan
Khiri Ket
3

Soi Patak 20

⊗⊗
7 8

Soi Patak 18

D

KARON

4028

Th Patak East

1

2

Karon Dragon Statue ◉ 4

Soi The Old Phuket

9 ⊗

Hat Karon ◉ 1

3

ANDAMAN SEA

Big Buddha Hike (1.5km

4

Sunrise Divers ●

Soi Patak 14

Karon Plaza

⊗ 6

Th Luang Phor Chuan

4028

Th Patak East

⊗ 5

5

For reviews see
◉	Experiences	p73
⊗	Eating	p74
☐	Shopping	p75

Dive Asia ● ☐ 11

Ⓝ 0   500
0   0.25 miles

Th Thai Na

6

A   **B**   **C**   **D**

Experiences

Hat Karon BEACH

⊙ MAP P72, B3

This 4km-long west-coast stretch of squeaky-fine sand is popular with families and, while it does get busy, there's always plenty of space to spread out. (หาดกะรน)

The Spa SPA

2 ⊙ MAP P72, B1

Rooms trail off a tree-shaded tropical garden and bowls of frangipanis lie strewn around: this is one of Karon's most ambience-filled spas. Your mind will be revitalised and your body scrubbed with tamarind, wrapped in coconut and given a glow with Dead Sea salts. Get romantic with 2½-hour couples'

Big Buddha Hike

From Karon's Soi Patak 14 (opposite Karon Plaza), a challenging, very worthwhile one-hour, 2.5km hike climbs through the lush jungle to **Big Buddha** (p76).

packages (6700B). (☎076 396139; www.movenpick.com; Mövenpick Resort, 509 Th Karon/Patak West; massage or treatment 1500-2000B; ⊙9am-9pm)

Wat Suwan Khiri Ket BUDDHIST TEMPLE

3 ⊙ MAP P72, C1

Set back from the road is this relatively new, impeccably maintained

Karon Dragon Statue (p74)

Surfing & Diving

During the April-to-October low season, you can take surf lessons (one hour 1200B) and rent surfboards/bodyboards (300/150B per hour) at the south end of Hat Karon. Recommended Karon dive operators include **Dive Asia** (Map p72, B6; ☑076 330598; www.diveasia.com; 23/6 Th Karon/Patak West; 2-/3-dive trip 3400/3900B; ☉10am-9pm) and **Sunrise Divers** (Map p72, C5; ☑076 398040, 084 626 4646; www.sunrise-divers.com; 269/24 Th Patak East; 3-dive trip 3700B, liveaboard from 4900B per day; ☉10am-6pm daily Nov-Apr, to 4pm Mon-Fri May-Oct).

temple complex with a small shrine occupied by a seated, black-stone Buddha. Next door stands the striking tiered-roof crematorium, open only on ceremonial days. The grounds are lush with banana, palm and mango trees. It's popular for its Tuesday and Friday **night market** (from 4pm) full of clothes and food stalls. (วัดสุวรรณคีรีเขต; Th Patak East; admission free; ☉5am-10pm)

Karon Dragon Statue   STATUE

4 ◉ MAP P72, B2

Perched by the central section of the beach, Karon's golden statue is often thought to embody the fabled sleeping dragon that, according

to local Chinese folklore, formed the island. It may also represent the Buddhist *naga,* a mythical half-human, half-cobra being. (ปู่พญานาค ราชศรีสุทโธ; Th Karon/Patak West)

Eating

Pad Thai Shop   THAI $

5 ✕ MAP P72, D6

This glorified roadside food shack makes absurdly good *kôw pàt þoo* (fried rice with crab), *pàt see-éw* (fried noodles), chicken stew and noodle soup. It also serves up some of the best *pàt tai* we've tasted: spicy and sweet, packed with tofu, egg and peanuts, and plated with spring onions, bean sprouts and lime. Don't miss the house-made chilli sauces. (Th Patak East; mains 50-80B; ☉8am-6pm Sat-Thu)

Eat Bar & Grill   GRILL $$$

6 ✕ MAP P72, C5

Expect awesome burgers and superb steaks, perhaps the best on Phuket, at this laid-back, busy grill specialist with a wooden bar, concrete walls and limited space (book ahead). The menu includes other dishes, but beef is the thing: prepared to your taste, stylishly presented and fairly priced, given the quality. Proper cocktails and coffee too. (☑085 292 5652; www.eatbargrill.com; 250/1 Th Patak East; mains 200-900B; ☉11am-10pm Mon-Sat; ☎)

Elephant Café by Tan
THAI, INTERNATIONAL **$$**

 MAP P72, C1

Reliable and popular spot for both Thai and Western food, near Karon's temple. Dine on curries and spicy salads, or steaks, chops and pizza, in the enclosed, garden-like interior. Plenty of vegetarian choices too, as well as cakes and cocktails. (076 398129; www.facebook.com/elephant cafe2005; 489 Th Patak East; mains 30-390B; 10am-11pm;)

Mr Coffee
CAFE **$$**

 MAP P72, C1

A popular Italian-run roadside cafe tucked away near Karon's temple. Home-baked cakes and pastries, cooked breakfasts, ciabatta and focaccia sandwiches and fruit shakes in jam jars (try a Cool Now: mango, mint, pineapple and cucumber) are served in a small concrete courtyard, and of course, there's quality espresso. (www.facebook.com/mr.coffephuket; 479/1 Th Patak East; meals 130-250B; 7.30am-10.30pm Mon-Sat Nov-Apr, 8am-4pm Mon-Sat May-Oct;)

Highway Curry
NORTH INDIAN **$$**

 MAP P72, D3

For a break from Thai flavours, this low-key, orange-walled, Indian-owned restaurant with helpful staff and wooden tables by the roadside rustles up delicately spiced North Indian curries mopped up with doughy nan. There's an impressive vegetarian selection, from samosas and pakora to *aloo jeera, shahi paneer* and *chana masala*. Also does takeaway. (083 024 3015; www.highwaycurry.com; 375/2 Th Patak East; mains 180-320B; 11am-11pm;)

Shopping

Lemongrass House
COSMETICS

10 MAP P72, B1

A branch of Phuket's favourite homegrown, organic-beauty brand. Stock up on rose-infused salt scrubs, green-tea face creams, jasmine moisturisers and all-natural citronella-and-lavender mosquito repellents – plus pet products! (088 761 4361; www.lemongrasshousethailand.com; 603 Th Patak East; 10.30am-10.30pm)

Baru
FASHION & ACCESSORIES

11 MAP P72, B6

A stunning collection of exotic prints, light fabrics, sparkly accessories, leather bags, elegant dresses and bold-coloured bikinis make Baru a hit with its fashion-loving devotees. This is what Phuket's signature East-meets-West island style is all about. (076 333237; www.barufashion.com; Th Karon/Patak West; 10am-11pm)

Worth a Trip 👀
Big Buddha

You've seen Big Buddha popping up from across the southern half of the island. At 45m tall, this awe-inspiring statue basks in some of Phuket's most glorious views from atop the Nakkerd Hills. It can feel more tourist attraction than spiritual haven, but the Buddha's sheer size and beauty, hilltop serenity and unbelievably gorgeous panoramas are reason enough to linger.

พระใหญ่

www.mingmongkolphuket.
com

off Rte 4021

admission free

🕐6am-7pm; 🅿

The Buddha

The peacefulness among tinkling bells, fluttering prayer notes and Buddhist flags flapping in the wind gives the place a powerful energy. Before climbing the stairs to the Buddha itself, pay your respects at the tin-roofed golden shrine. Construction began on Big Buddha in 2007 and is still very much ongoing. Funded exclusively by donations, he's dressed in Burmese alabaster, which isn't cheap, with a total price tag of around 100 million baht.

Phuketians refer to Big Buddha as Phuket's most important project in the last 100 years, which means a lot considering that construction on Phuket hasn't stopped for the last 20 years.

The Views

From the Buddha's view-laden plateau, peer into Kata's turquoise bay, spot the shimmering Karon strand and, to the southeast, count the islets dotting Chalong Bay. On the drive up, you'll meander past swirls of jungle and terraced banana groves.

The Hike

From Karon, a challenging and rewarding hike of 2.5km (one hour) leads up the jungle-cloaked hillside to almost the top of the Big Buddha access road. This well-signposted route starts on Soi Patak 14, opposite Karon Plaza. The road forks soon after, then a steep dirt path branches uphill to reach a clearing with a rest spot; from here, continue climbing through the shady jungle, with ropes on hand to help pull you up.

★ **Top Tips**

o As with all religious sites, dress conservatively. Women, especially, should cover up past the knee and over the shoulders. If needed, you'll be loaned a shawl and/or skirt.

o Don't miss the viewpoint hidden in the rocks just off the exit stairs.

o Beat the crowds by arriving early.

✕ **Take a Break**

About 450m below Big Buddha, **Star Mountain Sunset** (☎089 287 7577; off Rte 4021; mains 80-300B; ⊙8am-7pm) serves tasty Thai and international staples at tables with sweeping views across Phuket's southwest coast.

★ **Getting There**

🚗Drivers: it's 5.5km west off Rte 4021, 1km north of Chalong Circle.

🚗From Kata/Karon taxis cost 500B.

🚶A strenuous hike up from Karon (2.5km; one hour).

Explore
Hat Kata

Classier than Karon and without Patong's seedy hustle, Hat Kata (หาดกะตะ) attracts travellers of all kinds to its lively, beautiful, white-gold twin beaches. A prime spot for surfing in the shoulder and monsoon seasons, Kata also has terrific spas, good food, a highly rated yoga studio and a buzzing water sports scene.

The Short List

○ **Hat Kata (p83)** Sun-soaking on Kata's two beautiful golden beaches.

○ **Water Sports (p85)** Taking to the water with a kayak or paddleboard, diving into the deep, or surfing Kata Yai's waves.

○ **Spa Sensations (p83)** Lazing the days away between Thai massages, hydrating facials and mango body scrubs.

○ **Kata Cuisine (p84)** Dining in style at hidden-away Thai cheapies or super-star seafront global eateries, or joining a cooking class.

Getting There & Around

🚗 To/from airport (1200B), Phuket Town (600B), Patong (500B), Karon (300B).

🚌 Phuket Smart Bus to/from airport (170B, hourly), west coast beaches and Rawai. Minibus from airport (200B).

Sŏrng·tǎa·ou Passenger pick-up trucks to/from Phuket Town (40B, 7am to 5pm).

Hat Kata Map on p82

Karon Viewpoint (p84) THAISIGN/SHUTTERSTOCK ©

Walking Tour 🥾

Kata for Families

Largely free of the seediness that seeps into neighbouring Patong and, to a lesser extent, Karon, Kata is a great spot for families, packed with water sports, good food and family-oriented fun. This mostly waterfront walk allows you to dip in and out of its many popular activities while enjoying its two powdery beaches.

Walk Facts

Start Dino Park

End Hat Kata Noi

Length 3.5km; six hours

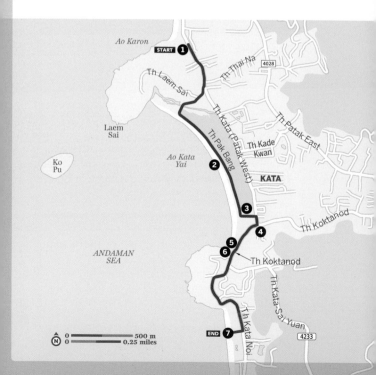

❶ Dino Park

Start at the northern end of town, where Kata meets Karon, and **Dino Park** (076 330625; www.dinopark. com; Th Karon/Patak West; adult/child 240/180B; 10am-11pm) offers minigolf in *Jurassic Park*–inspired gardens; if you don't fancy playing, just wander the grounds.

❷ Hat Kata Yai

Head south and downhill along Th Kata (Patak West), passing boutiques and souvenir shops, then turn right (west) on Th Pak Bang until you hit the sparkling white sands of **Hat Kata Yai** (p83). Stroll south down the beach, taking in the views of lush little Ko Pu looming on the horizon, and perhaps stopping for a dip or a sun-soak.

❸ Surf House

Continuing on, you'll reach **Surf House** (081 979 7737; www. surfhousephuket.com; 4 Th Pak Bang; 1hr surf slide 1000B; 9am-midnight;), an artificial-wave complex where kids can practise their wakeboarding moves while parents relax in the bar-restaurant. Alternatively, save the wave action for a little later.

❹ Caffeine Kick

If you're craving caffeine by this stage, take a quick detour inland to **Italian Job** (p86) for an espresso; it's a five-minute walk east along Th Pak Bang, then south on Th Kata (Patak West).

❺ Water Sports

At the rocky far southern end of Kata Yai you'll spot bobbing long-tail boats and a couple of laid-back water-sports outfitters, including **Nautilus Dive & Surf Shop** (076 330229; www.phuket surfing.com; 186/1 Th Kata Noi; class 1200B, board rental per hour/day 200/800B; 9am-6pm); drop in to hire kayaks, paddleboards and bodyboards, or, during the April-to-November low season, take a one-hour surf class among Kata's famous waves.

❻ Simple Seafood

Time for a bite to eat: this southern corner of Kata Yai is home to a clutch of cheap-and-cheerful sand-side seafood shacks well suited to families. Settle in at **Kata Mama** (p86) or **Kata BBQ** (www. facebook.com/katabbq; Hat Kata Yai; meals 80-350B; 8am-10.30pm;) for classic Thai stir-fries, curries and grilled seafood, served with prime Andaman views.

❼ Hat Kata Noi

From here, it's a 15-minute walk south and over the hill on Th Kata Noi to glimmering **Hat Kata Noi** (p83) – not in itself the most exciting stroll, but absolutely worth it when you spy the blonde sands on the other side.

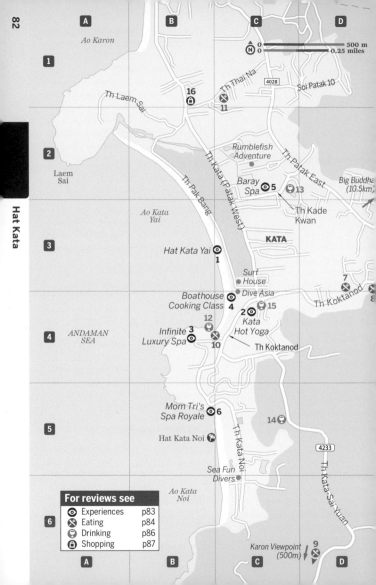

Hat Kata

Ao Karon

Th Thai Na

16

11

4028

Soi Patak 10

Th Laem Sai

Th Pak Bang

Th Kata (Patak West)

Laem
Sai

*Rumblefish
Adventure*

Th Patak East

Big Buddha
(10.5km)

Baray
Spa ⊙ 5

13

Th Kade
Kwan

Ao Kata
Yai

KATA

Hat Kata Yai ⊙
1

*Surf
House*

7

Dive Asia

Boathouse
Cooking Class ⊙
4

15

Th Koktanod

ANDAMAN
SEA

12

Kata ⊙ 2
Hot Yoga

Infinite 3
Luxury Spa ⊙

10

Th Koktanod

Mom Tri's
Spa Royale ⊙ 6

14

Hat Kata Noi

4233

*Sea Fun
Divers*

Th Kata Noi

Th Kata-Sai-Yuan

**Ao Kata
Noi**

Karon Viewpoint
(500m)

9

For reviews see
⊙ Experiences   p83
⊗ Eating   p84
⊖ Drinking   p86
⊟ Shopping   p87

N

0   500 m
0   0.25 miles

Experiences

Hat Kata Yai BEACH

1 ⊙ MAP P82, C3

Hat Kata is carved in two by a jutting headland. Blonde Hat Kata Yai (known as the main Kata beach) lies on the north side, while **Hat Kata Noi** (หาดกะตะน้อย) unravels to the south. Both are stunning and popular beaches; Kata Noi is a little more sheltered, while Kata Yai is the one to head to if you want to surf. (หาดกะตะใหญ่)

Kata Hot Yoga YOGA

2 ⊙ MAP P82, C4

Craving more heat? At Kata Hot Yoga, Bikram's famous asana series is taught over 90 minutes in a sweltering room by the expert owner and a roster of visiting international instructors. There are two to three classes daily. All levels welcome; no bookings needed. Multiclass packages offer good deals. (☑076 605950; www.katahotyoga.com; 217 Th Koktanod; 1/10 classes 550/3850B; ⏰classes 9am, 5.15pm & 7.15pm Mon-Fri, 9am & 5.15pm Sat & Sun)

Infinite Luxury Spa SPA

3 ⊙ MAP P82, B4

Tucked into Kata's most fashionable **luxury resort** (d 21,400-33,200B; P 🌀 🛜 🌊) and open to nonguests, this innovative, ubermodern spa blends traditional therapies and organic Ila products with bang-up-to-date technology that includes an antijetlag pod, a temperature-controlled bed and a colour-changing 'chakra room'. Treatments range from Thai massage to bio-energy mud-wraps, couples' oil massages and 'rainforest-rejuvenation' facials. Pricey, but perfect for a special-occasion splurge. (☑076 370777; www.katarocks.com; Kata Rocks, 186/22 Th Koktanod; treatment 3600-9500B; ⏰10am-10pm)

Boathouse Cooking Class COOKING

4 ⊙ MAP P82, C4

Kata's top fine-dining restaurant (p84) offers fantastic four-course, one-day and two-day Thai cooking classes, taking in a trip to the local market. (☑076 330015; www.boathouse-phuket.com; 182 Th Koktanod; classes 2570-4450B; ⏰hours vary)

Baray Spa SPA

5 ⊙ MAP P82, C2

Hidden away in a lush tropical garden full of interwoven canals and gushing waterfalls, this is a quality spa with a sophisticated, romantic edge. Keep it classic with a traditional Thai massage or spice things up with a full-body coffee scrub, a seaweed bust-firming treatment or a rehydrating facial. (☑076 330979; www.phuketsawasdee.com; Sawasdee Village, 38 Th Kade Kwan; massage or treatment 1200-5000B; ⏰10am-10pm)

Mom Tri's Spa Royale SPA

6 ⊙ MAP P82, B5

With organic spa products, trickling water features, seaside treatment

Karon Viewpoint

From the majestic clifftop lookout of **Karon Viewpoint** (จุดชม วิวกะรน; Map p80, C6; Rte 4233), views sweep across Kata to the northern reaches of Karon and, to the south, wrap around the coast to Laem Phromthep. Come for sunset, though it's a beautiful spot at any time. It's 3km south of central Kata on Rte 4233. Don't linger late at night. There have been reports of attacks and robberies in the wee hours.

rooms and highly skilled therapists, this luxury hotel spa atop the rocks on northern Kata Noi is one of southern Phuket's finest spas. The soothing 90-minute cucumber wrap (4000B) is a godsend if you've notched up a few too many hours under the sun. (☑076 333568; www.villaroyalephuket.com; Mom Tri's Villa Royale, 12 Th Kata Noi, Hat Kata Noi; massage or treatment 1500-5500B; ⏰10am-7pm)

Eating

Red Duck   THAI $$

7 ⊗ MAP P82, D3

Dishes at this hidden-away eatery with a tiny terrace are more expensive than at Kata's other Thai restaurants, but they're delicious, MSG-free but prepared with the freshest of ingredients. The seafood curries and soups are especially

fine. Many of the Thai classics can be done in vegan version, such as beautifully spiced massaman or vegetable larb. Service is excellent. (☑084 850 2929; www.facebook.com/redduckrestaurant; 88/3 Th Koktanod; mains 240-380B; ⏰noon-11pm, closed Mon May-Sep; 🛜🍽)

Boathouse   INTERNATIONAL $$$

It's all very glam at the luxurious, beachside **Boathouse** (d incl breakfast 9000-39,000B; 🅿❄🛜🍽) (see 4 ⊙ Map p82, C4), one of Phuket's most respected restaurants. The Thai/Mediterranean food (garlic-grilled tiger prawns, lamb-shank massaman, Australian-beef-tenderloin carpaccio) is fabulous, the wine list famously expansive, the service attentive and the sea views sublime. Special sharing platters are prepared at your table, and there are daily-changing set menus (930B to 1750B). (mains 250-1500B; ⏰noon-11pm)

Istanbul Restaurant   TURKISH $$

8 ⊗ MAP P82, D3

This delightful, family-run place is the most popular foreign restaurant in Kata and for good reason. The food is simply splendid, ranging from big Western- or Turkish-style breakfasts to completely authentic and supertasty mains such as *hünkar beğendi* (beef stew on a bed of eggplant puree), kebabs and Turkish *pide*. Then there are the superb soups, salads and delectable desserts. (☑091 820 7173; www.istanbulrestaurantphuket.

com; 100/87 Th Koktanod; meals 120-320B; ☹9am-10pm Tue-Sat)

Sabai Corner INTERNATIONAL, THAI $$

9 MAP P82, D6

There's no better Phuket view than the one you'll glimpse from Sabai Corner's wide deck: all the way to Karon in one direction and an endless horizon of blue ocean rippling around the island in the other. The food isn't bad either, from fried rice, grilled fish and searing Thai curries, to salads, pastas and popular wood-fired pizza.

From Kata, head 3km south towards Rawai/Hat Nai Han on Rte 4233, turn downhill right behind Karon Viewpoint and drive 1.5km. (☎089 875 5525; www.sabaicorner phuket.com; Soi Laem Mum Nai, off Rte 4233; mains 160-490B; ☹10am-10pm; 🛜)

Kata Rocks Clubhouse INTERNATIONAL, THAI $$$

The divine setting alone is enough to seek out this poolside restaurant at design-led Kata Rocks (see 3 ◉ Map p82, B4)), where the sparkling Andaman wraps around a rocky headland. The Thai-Mediterranean cooking is excellent too, from pizzas, pastas, grilled meats and health-focused salads to classic Phuketian *mŏo hong* (pepper-and-garlic-braised pork). Beautifully mixed cocktails (390B to 490B). (☎076 370777; www.katarocks.com; 186/22 Th Koktanod; mains 350-1600B; ☹6.30-10.30am, 11am-5.30pm & 6pm-midnight; 🛜🍽)

Kata Water Sports

Both of Kata's beaches offer decent surfing from April to November; one-hour private classes costs 1200B and board rental 200/800B per hour/day. Hiring SUP kit or kayaks costs 300/900B per hour/day. Among Kata's well-established dive schools are **Sea Fun Divers** (Map p80, C6; ☎076 330124; www.seafun divers.com; Katathani, 14 Th Kata Noi; 2-/3-dive trip 3900/4400B; ☹9am-6pm), **Dive Asia** (Map p80, C4; ☎076 330598; www.diveasia.com; 1/21 Th Pak Bang; 2-/3-dive trip 3400/3900B; ☹9am-9pm) and **Rumblefish Adventure** (Map p80, C2; ☎095 441 8665; www.rumblefishadventure.com; 98/79 Beach Centre, Th Kata/Patak West; 2-dive trip 3500-4500B; ☹9am-7pm).

Mom Tri's Kitchen FUSION, MEDITERRANEAN $$$

A special-occasion or intimate-lunch splash-out spot, Mom Tri's Kitchen revolves around fine wines, fusion haute cuisine and views of beautiful Hat Kata Noi from a sensational cliff-side perch (see 6 ◉ Map p82, B5). Diners pick from a menu that loops seasonal, local ingredients into exquisite Mediterranean-fuelled dishes, as well as Thai classics with a European twist, like snapper tempura, rock-lobster ravioli and lemongrass-infused sea bass. (mains 540-1400B; ⏰11am-11pm; P ⚲)

Kata Mama

THAI $

10 🍴 MAP P82, C4

Our pick of several cheapie seafood places at the southern end of Hat Kata Yai, long-standing Kata Mama keeps busy thanks to its charming management, reliably tasty Thai standards and low-key sand-side setting on a prime patch of beach. (Hat Kata Yai; mains 100-200B; ⏰8.30am-9.30pm)

Kwong Shop Seafood

THAI, SEAFOOD $$

11 🍴 MAP P82, C1

Who doesn't love a time-worn fish shack? Using enticing displays of fresh seafood and snaps of blissed-out diners as bait, this old-school Thai joint has been reeling in hungry customers for over 25 years. It's cheap and cheerful, and its walls make a visual feast of coins and notes. (65/1 Th Thai Na; mains 80-250B; ⏰10am-midnight; 📶)

Drinking

Ska Bar

BAR

12 🍺 MAP P82, B4

Tucked into the rocks on the southernmost curl of Hat Kata Yai and seemingly intertwined with the trunk of a grand old banyan tree, laid-back, Rasta-vibe Ska is our choice for seaside sundowners, served by welcoming Thai bartenders. Buoys, paper lanterns

and flags dangle from the canopy, and there are often fire shows. (www.skabar-phuket.com; 186/12 Th Koktanod; ⏰1pm-2am)

Art Space Cafe & Gallery

BAR

13 🍺 MAP P82, C2

Hands down the most fabulously quirky bar in Phuket, this trippy, multiuse space bursts with colour and is smothered in uniquely brushed canvases and sculptures celebrating, especially, the feminine form. It's the work of the creative Mr Pan and his tattoo-artist wife, who whip up both cocktails and veggie meals (160B to 400B). There's normally live music around 8pm. (📞090 156 0677; Th Kade Kwan; ⏰noon-midnight)

After Beach Bar

BAR

14 🍺 MAP P82, C5

It's impossible to overstate how glorious the views are from this thatched reggae bar clinging to a cliff above Kata: rippling sea, rocky peninsulas and palm-sprinkled hills. Throw in Bob Marley tunes and you have the perfect sunset-watching spot. When the sun finally drops, fishing-boat lights blanket the horizon. Try the *pàt tai* (mains 100B to 400B). (📞084 745 9365; Rte 4233; ⏰11am-10pm)

Italian Job

CAFE

15 🍺 MAP P82, C4

A contemporary-style Italian coffee lounge with wi-fi, pastries, delicious espresso, limoncello (Italian lemon liqueur) and a loyal morning following (coffees 60B to 130B). It overlooks a busy junction – perfect for people-watching from air-conditioned comfort. Sometimes closed for a time in low season (May to October). (☏098 708 3843; www.facebook.com/italianjobcoffeekata; 179/1 Th Koktanod; ⏰8am-midnight Dec-Mar, to 4pm Apr-Nov; 🛜)

Shopping

Siam Handicraft CLOTHING

16 🔒 MAP P82, B1

Handwoven linen dresses, shirts, shawls, trousers and other men's and women's fashion, mostly locally made with hemp and organic cotton, are the speciality at this boho boutique, which also stocks a lovely collection of silver and beaded jewellery and handmade shoes. (www.facebook.com/siamhandicraft.phuket; 12-14 Th Karon/Patak West; ⏰10am-10pm Mon-Sat)

La Banana FASHION & ACCESSORIES

Because one bikini is never enough. Drop into this teensy boutique (see 16 🔒 Map p82, B1) to stock up on skimpy, affordable two-pieces in a rainbow of colours, styles and patterns, plus floaty beachwear and dresses for casually draping over the top. Also in northern Karon. (Th Kata/Patak West; ⏰11am-11pm)

Hat Kata Noi (p83)

Explore
Rawai

Rawai (ราไวย์) is a delightful place to stay, live or explore. This laid-back stretch of Phuket's south coast is teeming with retirees, artists and Thai and expat entrepreneurs, plus relaxed cafes and plenty of yoga and moo·ay tai (Thai boxing). The region is defined not just by its beautiful salt-white beaches but also by its lush coastal hills, which rise steeply and tumble into the Andaman Sea forming Laem Phromthep. Despite the development you can still feel nature, especially on the beach.

The Short List

○ **Laem Phromthep (p90)** Watching the sun sink over the island's southernmost tip.

○ **Coffee culture (p95)** Mooching among Phuket's most relaxed cafes.

○ **Moo·ay tai (p94)** Learning the ropes of Thai boxing.

○ **Kitesurfing & Yoga (p93)** Skimming the waves or easing into asanas.

○ **Seafood grills (p96)** Feasting on simple, super-fresh seafood.

Getting There & Around

🚗 Rawai/Hat Nai Han to airport (1000B), Patong (700B) and Phuket Town (500B).

🚌 Phuket Smart Bus to airport via west-coast beaches (50B to 170B, hourly 6am to 8.15pm).

Sŏrng·tăa·ou To/from Phuket Town (30B, 7am to 5.30pm) and Hat Nai Han (40B, 8am to 6pm).

Rawai Map on p92

Long-tail boats, Hat Rawai (p94) ADRIAN BAKER/SHUTTERSTOCK ©

Top Experience 📷
Laem Phromthep

This is it: Phuket's southernmost point. If you want to see the luscious Andaman shimmer around the island into the distance, come to outrageously scenic Laem Phromthep. You won't be alone, but once you scan the 270 degrees of Andaman Sea elegantly arching around the rocky cape below, where local fishers cast into the whooshing waves, that won't even matter.

◉ MAP P92, C4

แหลมพรหมเทพ

Rte 4233

The Views

There's a reason why busloads of tourists and packs of Phuketians descend on buzzy Laem Phromthep every afternoon. From the hilltop viewpoint, you'll enjoy panoramic vistas over the southern tip of Phuket, northwest to Hat Nai Han (p93) and across the tropical turquoise waters of the island-dotted Andaman. But the pink-tinged sunset is the real reason to visit. People sprawl and pose on the grass or atop the palm-lined concrete wall to bask in the final moments of warmth, before the sun drops into the sea.

Elephant Shrine

On the central platform above the cape's car park sits a small, atmospheric elephant shrine encircled by hundreds of wooden, ceramic and gold-painted elephant statues of all sizes, adorned with vibrantly coloured flower garlands. The elephants represent wisdom and strength in Buddhist teaching, and local believers pray here.

Lighthouse

Topped by two golden elephants, Laem Phromthep's lighthouse was built in 1996 to commemorate the Golden Jubilee of King Bhumibol Adulyadej. From the very top you'll gain an elevated view of the sunset and, usually, more exciting photo opportunities away from the crowds. On the lighthouse door there's a handy information board detailing the day's sunrise and sunset times.

★ Top Tips

o At sunset, masses of tour buses pack on to the cape; arrive by 4pm to beat the crowds, then pop back for sunset.

o Take the steep downhill fishermen's trail to reach the rocky peninsula jutting out into the sea below and watch the sun drop in a more peaceful environment.

o For a quieter sunset-watching experience, find the **Windmill Viewpoint** (จุดชมวิว กังหันลม; Rte 4233), 1.5km north of Laem Phromthep.

✗ Take a Break

Head to Unni's (p96) on nearby Hat Nai Han.

Make a pilgrimage to the popular seafood grills (p93) along the waterfront at Hat Rawai.

★ Getting There

Unless you fancy a steep hike, you'll need your own wheels to reach Laem Phromthep; it's 3km southwest of Hat Rawai.

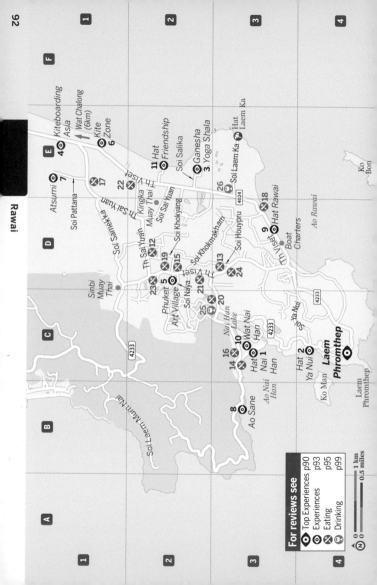

Rawai

Kiteboarding Asia
Kite Zone 4
6
Wat Chalong (6km)

11 Hat Friendship
Ganesha 3 Yoga Shala
Soi Salika
Hat Laem Ka

Atsumi 7
17
22
Kingka Muay Thai
Th Viset
Th Sai Yuan
Soi Sai Yuan
26
Hat Rawai 18
9
Ko Bon

Soi Pattana
Soi Samakka
Th Sai Yuan
Soi Sai Yuan
Soi Khokyang
Soi Houypru
Soi Laem Ka

Ao Rawai

Soi Pattana
19 12
15
13
24
Soi Khokmakham
Th Viset
Boat Charters

Sinbi Muay Thai
23
Phuket 5 Art Village
21
20
25
Soi Naya
Th Viset

4024

4233

16
14
10 1
Nai Han Lake
Wat Nai Han

Ao Sane
Hat Nai Han
Ya Nui 2
Soi Ya Nui
4233

8

Ao Nai Han

Ko Man
Ya Nui

Laem Phromthep

Laem Phromthep

For reviews see	
●	Top Experiences p90
●	Experiences p93
✕	Eating p95
●	Drinking p99

0   1 km
0   0.5 miles

Experiences

Hat Nai Han
BEACH

MAP P92, C3

Ask a Phuketian or local expat for their favourite island beach and many will choose Hat Nai Han. A beautifully curved crescent on the west side of Laem Phromthep, backed by casuarinas and a seafront wát (temple), and washed by turquoise water, it remains one of Rawai's great swimming and sun-soaking spots (be careful of low-season riptides). (หาดในหาน)

Hat Ya Nui
BEACH

2 MAP P92, C4

About 700m north of Laem Phromthep, tucked between the cape and Hat Nai Han where the road dips down to the sea, is this gorgeous mellow cove with a healthy, rocky snorkelling reef. Hat Ya Nui is the quintessential turquoise bay, with honey-coloured sand, jungly mountains behind and an island dominating the horizon. It's a deservedly popular sunset-watching spot. (หาดยะนุ้ย; Rte 4233)

Ganesha Yoga Shala
YOGA

3 MAP P92, E2

Led by one of Phuket's top yoga teachers, Julie Hirunchai, this well-established studio near southern Hat Friendship (off Rte 4024) specialises in Mysore Ashtanga yoga. There's a daily drop-in 1½-hour class (except on Saturday), with levels varying by day. Mats, towels and water are provided; check the latest schedules online. (089 868 2639; www.ganeshayogaphuket.com; 25/7 Soi Salika, Th Viset; class 350B; Sun-Fri)

Kiteboarding Asia
KITESURFING

4 MAP P92, E1

This efficient, professional kite-surfing outfit has outlets across Thailand. On Phuket, its Rawai branch offers kit rental (per hour/day 1400/4000B) and IKO-certified courses from November to April; during the monsoon it operates from its branch (p131) on Hat Nai Yang. There are also wakeboarding lessons (one hour 1000B). (081 591 4594; www.kiteboardingasia.com; 26/4 Th Viset; 1-/3-day course 4000/11,000B; 9am-6pm Nov-Apr)

Phuket Art Village
ARTS CENTRE

5 MAP P92, D2

A group of talented Thai artists has come together to set up this bohemian arts commune, just off Rawai's main strip. Feel free to wander the wonderfully creative home-studio-galleries packed with boldly contemporary original artwork and, if you're lucky, meet some of the eight resident artists. (หมู่บ้านศิลปะ ภูเก็ต; www.facebook.com/pages/Phuket-Art-Village/320158668080202; 28/68 Soi Naya 2; admission free; 8am-10pm, hours vary)

Kite Zone
KITESURFING

6 MAP P92, E1

This cool young multilingual kite-surfing school has a tremendous

Rawai Moo·ay Tai

Rawai is the epicentre of Phuket's ever-growing *moo·ay tai* (Thai boxing, also spelt *muay Thai*) mania, home to half a dozen schools where students live and train in camps with professional *moo·ay tai* fighters. Popular schools include **Kingka Supa Muay Thai** (Map p90, D2; ☎076 226495; www.kingkamuaythai.com; 43/42 Mu 7, Soi Sai Yuan, Th Viset; per session/week 600/3000B; ⏰7am-7pm), **Sinbi Muay Thai** (Map p90, D1; ☎093 690 3322; www.sinbi-muaythai.com; 100/15 Mu 7, Th Sai Yuan; per session/week 400/3000B; ⏰7.30am-6pm Mon-Sat, from 9am Sun) and, in Chalong, **Tiger Muay Thai** (☎076 367071; www.tigermuay-thai.com; 7/35 Mu 5, Soi Taiad; per session/week 500/3500B; ⏰7am-7pm Mon-Sat).

perch on Hat Friendship. IKO-certified courses range from one-hour private tasters to three-day, 10-hour courses. From April to October, classes happen at Hat Nai Yang (p91) on the northwest side of the island. Also has some accommodation (700B to 1400B), rents kit (per hour/day 1200/3500B) and runs stand-up paddle trips (from 700B). (☎083 395 2005; www.kitesurfthailand.com; Hat Friendship; 1hr lesson 1600B, 3-day course 10,000-15,000B; ⏰hours vary)

Atsumi
SPA

7 MAP P92, E1

At this earthy fasting-detox retreat, guests check in for days-long water, juice and/or herb fasts with massages. But non-dieters are also welcome for yoga or spa sessions, taking in traditional Thai, oil and deep-tissue treatments, plus signature Thaiatsu (Thai meets shiatsu) massages. Day passes (2000B to 2500B) include yoga and pool access. Atsumi runs health-focused Raw Cafe Phuket (p98) nearby. (☎096 638 7654; www.atsumihealing.com; 34/18 Soi King Pattana 4, Th Sai Yuan; massage or treatment 600-1500B, detox package per day 7050-10,500B; ⏰7am-7pm, spa closed Wed)

Ao Sane
BEACH

8 MAP P92, B3

Just northwest from Hat Nai Han, on Rawai's west coast, you might well think the road dead ends. But power on, passing the **Nai Harn resort** (☎076 380 200; www.thenaiharn.com; 23/3 Mu 1, Hat Nai Han; d incl breakfast 6960-23,250B; P ❄ � 🟰) and (sadly) some new development, and you'll wind 500m along the dramatic coast to the small but beautiful, boulder-strewn white-sand beach of Ao Sane. It's rugged and laid-back, enticing regular return visitors. (อ่าวเสน)

Hat Rawai
BEACH

9 MAP P92, D3

Not really good for lounging, Hat Rawai is a shallow, rocky beach on

the east side of Laem Phromthep.
Its waters are used as a busy
long-tail and speedboat harbour,
while cheap-and-cheerful seafood
grills line its low-key promenade.
หาดราไวย์)

Wat Nai Han BUDDHIST MONASTERY

10 ⊙ MAP P92, C3

Tucked into the trees behind lovely
Hat Nai Han, this working seafront
monastery is partly responsible
for this area's lack of development.
If you show up at dawn you can
watch, or even join in, as the monks
chant scripture; ask permission
from a monk the day before. (วัด
ในหาน; Hat Nai Han; admission free;
⊙daylight hours)

Hat Friendship BEACH

11 ⊙ MAP P92, E2

A wide beach on Rawai's east
coast that's OK for swimming and
also popular with kitesurfers from
November to April. (หาดมิตรภาพ)

Eating

Rum Jungle INTERNATIONAL $$$

12 ✴ MAP P92, D2

Arguably Rawai's finest restaurant,
this semi-open, thatched-roof
spot with an exceptional world-
beat soundtrack serves elegant
Italian and international dishes in a
laid-back, intimate setting. Divine
made-from-scratch pasta sauces
are served alongside crisp salads,
fresh mussels and Australian beef
tenderloin doused in pepper sauce.

Tempting veggie choices include
aubergine parmigiana and pasta
Gorgonzola. Book ahead. (☏076
388153; www.facebook.com/rumjungle.
rawai.phuket; 69/8 Mu 1, Th Sai Yuan;
mains 190-690B; ⊙11am-3pm & 5.30-
11pm Mon-Sat Nov-Mar, 3-11pm Mon-Sat
Apr-Oct; 🛜✴)

Coffee Tribe CAFE $$

13 ✴ MAP P92, D3

Digital nomads and yoga and
moo·ay tai students converge at
this fashionably laid-back, health-
oriented cafe. The artistically

Wat Chalong

Dating back 150 years, **Wat
Chalong** (วัดฉลอง; Map p90, E1;
www.wat-chalong-phuket.com;
Rte 4021; admission by donation;
⊙7am-5pm; P) is Phuket's
busiest Buddhist temple. Its
three-tiered, salmon-pink, 61m-
high *chedi* (a later addition)
has 36 golden Buddhas seated,
reclining and meditating
around its elaborate exterior;
green-and-gold *naga* line the
banisters and the lotus ponds
behind, while at the top sits
what is said to be a fragment
of Buddha's bone. Busloads of
visitors pour in, so swing by in
the early morning for a chance
of tranquillity. It's 7km northeast of central Rawai.

Please dress respectfully;
skirts and shawls are provided
for those needing to cover up.

prepared dishes are all about fresh ingredients, some straight from the house garden. Tuck into smoothie bowls, egg-white omelettes, rye-bread sandwiches and organic granola with homemade yoghurt, plus expertly poured organic coffees. (☑076 388134; www.coffeetribe.co.th; 83/13 Mu 2, Th Viset; meals 150-290B; ⏰7am-6.30pm Fri-Wed)

Rock Salt
INTERNATIONAL $$$

14 MAP P92, C3

Waves lap the rocks below your table at this wonderfully scenic terrace restaurant overlooking northern Hat Nai Han. The creative Mediterranean-Thai menu has fun with seasonal, all-organic produce and global influences, crafting pea-pesto pasta, Rawai-seafood bouillabaisse and fish of the day, served steamed or wood-fired. Charcuterie, cheeses, breads and yoghurts are homemade, while the impressive wine list includes

---

Seafood Grills

Hat Rawai is lined with a dozen locally owned seafood grills sizzling fresh catch along the roadside (mains 90B to 300B) throughout the day, with seating on plastic chairs or at low tables with blankets on the floor. It doesn't really matter which one you choose. All the fish is fresh, as are the crab, clams, mussels, squid, lobster and tiger prawns.

Thai rosés. (☑076 380200; www.thenaiharn.com; 23/3 Mu 1, Th Viset, Hat Nai Han; mains 500-850B; ⏰7.30-10am & 12.30-11pm; 🛜🅿)

German Bakery
EUROPEAN $

15 MAP P92, D2

This fun, friendly, semi-outdoor restaurant run by a German-Thai couple does the best pastries in Rawai and remains a deservedly popular breakfast spot. It makes fine brown bread, excellent pineapple pancakes and French toast, and decent bratwurst and sauerkraut. (Th Viset; mains 80-200B; ⏰7.30am-4.30pm; 🅿)

Unni's
INTERNATIONAL $$

16 MAP P92, C3

Tucked back from Hat Nai Han, Phuket's cheerful branch of Ko Phi-Phi's much-loved Unni's (p141) delivers with its globe-trotting line-up of Buddha bowls, wraps, salads, burgers, Thai favourites and tapas (avocado-feta bruschetta, chicken satay), plated in a stylishly minimalist space with subway-tiled walls and a smattering of tables. All Thai dishes – from pàt tai to massaman and pá·naang curries – can be vegetarian. (☑091 837 5931; www.facebook.com/unnisnaiharn; 14/69 Mu 1, Hat Nai Han; mains 170-350B; ⏰7.30am-9pm; 🛜🅿)

Som Tum Lanna
THAI $$

17 MAP P92, E1

When it comes to sôm·dam (spicy green-papaya salad) at this Isan soul-food shack, order it mild – it'll still bring some serious heat. Salads, in a variety of versions, are pounded in an open-plan kitchen, while the fish, chicken and stir-fries are also good. (📞 081 597 0569; 3/7 Th Sai Yuan, Hat Rawai; mains 80-250B; ⏰ 10am-4pm Tue-Sun; 🅿)

Baan Rimlay
THAI $$

8 ✖ MAP P92, D3

This shady spot immediately south-west of Rawai's pier steams clams, mussels and fish, and grills squid, prawns and lobster to perfection. For something light, try the terrific seafood salads. Dishes here – including crab meat curry and tamarind prawns – are a tad pricier than at neighbouring options but you're paying for the seaside location. It can get busy with loud tour groups.

(📞 095 426 4494; Th Viset, Hat Rawai; mains 100-400B; ⏰ 10am-10pm; 🅿)

A Spoonful of Sugar
CAFE $$

19 ✖ MAP P92, D2

Practically everything is wholesome and tasty at this sweet, white-washed cafe coated in flower prints. Wholemeal pancakes are topped with mango or kiwi and yoghurt, omelettes are stuffed with veggies, and there's a long list of coffees, smoothies, mix-your-own juices and protein shakes. It's popular for breakfast. Laze in the air-con lounge or on the wraparound veranda. (📞 076 388432; www.facebook.com/spoonfulofsugar; 30/10 Mu 1, Th Viset; mains 90-180B; ⏰ 8am-7pm Tue-Sun Nov-Apr, to 5pm Mar-Oct; 🛜 📶)

Wat Chalong (p95)

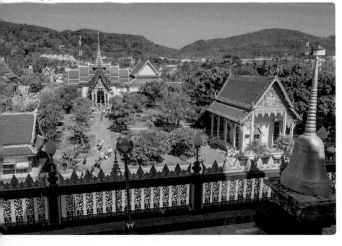

Boat Charters

Southern Phuket's outlying islands, such as Ko Bon and Coral Island, are easily visited by chartering a long-tail boat or a speedboat from Hat Rawai, though they're no secret these days. Rates vary depending on your bargaining skills, but might be around 1200/2400B to Ko Bon by long-tail/speedboat.

Natural Efe Macrobiotic World   VEGETARIAN $$

20 🍴 MAP P92, C2

This chilled-out health-food kitchen plates up such organic, sugar-free vegan delights as tofu sandwiches, dried-fruits-and-quinoa salad, lentil soup and breakfast bowls, at wooden tables set around an aqua pool in its leafy back courtyard. There's an all-you-can-eat organic Saturday and Sunday buffet (300B) in high season, as well as teas, freshly squeezed juices and health drinks (including hemp milk). (☑076 390301; www.macrobioticworld.com; 14/93-94 Mu 1, Th Viset; mains 140-300B; ⏰9am-9pm; 🛜🍽)

Delish Cafe   CAFE $$

21 🍴 MAP P92, D2

Gorgeous homemade breakfasts involving Chiang Rai coffee beans, Chiang Mai avocados, artisan jams, muesli-fruit bowls, stuffed croissants or French toast with zingy mango on home-baked bread are the draw at friendly Aussie-owned Delish, one of Rawai's wonderful cafes. Choose from the flower-fringed roadside terrace or cool air-con indoors. (☑076 388 149; www.facebook.com/DelishCafePhuket; 5/30 Th Viset; meals 140-210B; ⏰7.30am-5pm Mon-Sat; 🅿🛜)

Raw Cafe Phuket   HEALTH FOOD $$

22 🍴 MAP P92, E2

A popular roadside health-food cafe, where a creative, vegetarian-bliss menu of granola bowls, zucchini rolls, avocado salads, zucchini-almond burgers and brown-rice stir-fries is served in a minimalist wood-and-concrete space or on the flower-fringed back garden terrace. Fresh juices and smoothies are delicious too; try an Ultimate Cleanse with orange and watermelon. (☑076 298224; www.atsumirawcafe.com; 99/1 Mu 7, Th Viset; meals 150-280B; ⏰9am-8pm; 🛜🍽)

Gallery Cafe   CAFE $$

23 🍴 MAP P92, D2

A small branch of Phuket's astoundingly popular Gallery Cafe family, serving its winning formula of all-day breakfasts and international-Thai bites – mushroom-spinach omelettes, buttermilk pancakes, spiced French toast, smoothie bowls, light pastas, rice and noodle stir-fries and sparky fresh tropical juices. (☑076 602839; www.gallerycafephuket.com; 39/12 Th Sai Yuan; meals 140-350B; ⏰8am-5pm; 🛜🍽)

Number 1 Thai Food   THAI $

24 MAP P92, D3

Don't let the humble roots fool you. This delightful garden cafe-restaurant run out of the chef's front yard serves some delicious Thai food: searing *pá·naang* curry (clotted with coconut cream), sticky tamarind prawns, spicy fish soup and fresh fish of day. (83/40 Mu 2, Th Viset; mains 100-150B; ⏰4pm-midnight)

Drinking

Reggae Bar   BAR

25 🍺 MAP P92, C2

Spilling out from an old wooden shed, this cluttered lounge bobbing to classic roots tunes is a leathersmiths by day, and later hosts impromptu jams and erratic concerts, barbecues and parties, featuring local reggae bands and, occasionally, some of Thailand's most legendary Rastas. Art is plastered across walls and blacklight graffiti covers every inch of space. (Th Viset; ⏰noon-late, hours vary)

Nikita's   BAR

This long-running open-air hangout gazes over the sea just west of Rawai's pier (see 18 🍴 Map p92, D3) and offers reasonably priced beers and cocktails, as well as coffee, green tea and a good selection of shakes. A mango margarita, perhaps? If you're hungry, there are wood-fired pizzas, international mains and a lot of seafood (220B to 500B). (📞076 288703; www.nikitas-phuket.com; Hat Rawai; ⏰9.30am-11pm; 📶)

Chalong Bay Rum

Chalong, 9km north of Rawai, is home to Phuket's only working distillery. **Chalong Bay Rum** (ฉลองเบย์รัม ดิสทิลเลอรี่; 📞093 575 1119; www.chalongbayrum.com; 14/2 Mu 2, Soi Palai 2, off Th Chao Fa East; tour 450B; ⏰11am-10pm, tours hourly 2-6pm; 🅿) was launched by French couple Marine Lucchini and Thibault Spithakis. Upon arrival for the 30-minute tour, you'll be awarded a mojito concocted with their delicious product. The distillery also hosts two-hour cocktail workshops (Monday and Thursday; 1700B). Book ahead, mostly because you'll need directions; 3km northeast of Chalong Circle, turn right (east) at Phuket Zoo signs, then it's signposted shortly after.

Laguna Rawai Plaza   CLUB, BAR

26 🍺 MAP P92, E3

One of the few late-night spots in mellow Rawai, the Laguna club gets busy on weekend nights, attracting a mixed crowd of Thais, foreigners and bar girls. Opposite is a strip of bars where you can showcase your pool-playing skills. The bars are open until 2am, but sometimes run for longer; the club doesn't open until late. (📞098 031 2700; www.lagunarawai.com; 178/15 Mu 2, Th Viset; ⏰3pm-2am; 📶)

Explore

Hat Kamala

A mellow hybrid of grittier Karon and glitzier Surin, Kamala (หาดกมลา) is home to a large Muslim population, and lures in a mix of longer-term, low-key visitors, including families, retirees and young couples. The sweeping golden bay is magnificent and serene, with palms and pines mingling on its leafy, rocky northern end. The arrival of two beach clubs spells an upmarket swing – but for now at least, Kamala remains relatively laid-back.

The Short List

○ **Hat Kamala (p103)** Relaxing on honey-blonde, pine fringed sands, or tackling the surf.

○ **Beach Clubs (p105)** Finding Phuket fabulousness at the smattering of swanky beach clubs on northern Hat Kamala.

○ **Keemala resort (p103)** Escaping into the jungle-wrapped nearby hills for a spa treatment or an organic meal at this magical, ecoconscious resort.

○ **Tsunami Memorial (p103)** A poignant reminder of Kamala's past.

Getting There & Around

🚗 To/from airport (700B) and Surin (200B to 300B).

🚌 Phuket Smart Bus to/from airport (150B, hourly), west coast beaches and Rawai.

Sörng·tăa·ou Passenger pick-up trucks to/from Phuket Town (40B) and Surin (20B); 7am to 5pm.

Hat Kamala Map on p102

Hat Kamala (p103) DENIS COSTILLE/SHUTTERSTOCK ©

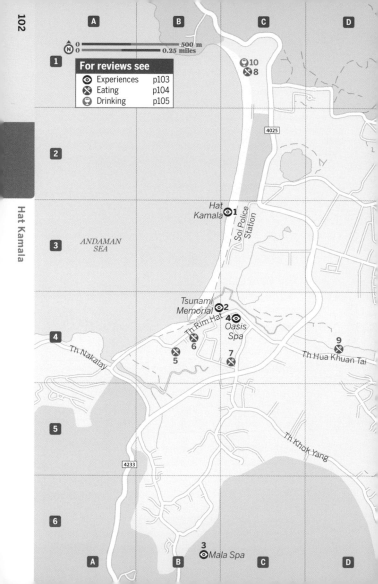

For reviews see

◉ Experiences p103
✕ Eating p104
🍷 Drinking p105

0 _____ 500 m
0 _____ 0.25 miles

🍷 10
✕ 8

ANDAMAN
SEA

Hat
Kamala ◉ 1

Soi Police Station

4025

Tsunami
Memorial ◉ 2

Th Rim Hat

✕ 6
✕ 5

4 ◉
Oasis
Spa

✕ 7

9 ✕
Th Hua Khuan Tai

Th Nakalay

Th Khok Yang

4233

3 ◉ Mala Spa

Experiences

Hat Kamala BEACH

◉ MAP P102, C3

Comparatively quiet and laid-back by Phuket standards, Hat Kamala is a well-enclosed white strand with a mostly rustic feel, framed between green-clad headlands and a spectacular turquoise bay, with a couple of glitzy beach clubs now buzzing at its northern end. (หาดกมลา)

Tsunami Memorial MEMORIAL

2 ◉ MAP P102, B4

Kamala was one of Phuket's worst-hit areas during the 2004 Boxing Day tsunami. The 2006 Heart of the Universe Memorial pays tribute to lost loved ones with a moving, wave-inspired metallic oval created by

Kamala Surfing

During the May to October monsoon, you can hire surfboards (300B per hour) and paddleboards (400B per hour) and take surf classes (1500B).

prominent Thai artist Udon Jiraksa, set in a small palm-sprinkled park. (อนุสรณ์สถานสึนามิ)

Mala Spa SPA

3 ◉ MAP P102, B6

Expert therapists and organic, cruelty-free products are combined to deliver sensational, tradition-meets-innovation treatments at this fabulous spa, set within the

Tsunami Memorial

Phuket Fantasea

It's impossible to ignore the brochures, touts and tour operators flogging Phuket Fantasea, the US$60 million 'cultural theme park' just east of Hat Kamala, promoted as one of the island's top 'family-friendly' attractions. While it's very popular with tour groups, we recommend reading up on the serious animal-welfare issues associated with this Vegas-style spectacle, at which animals are forced to 'perform' daily.

fairy-tale-like Keemala resort (p145), 2km inland (south) from Kamala. Massages, facials, body scrubs and wraps, aromatherapy baths and healing therapies happen in oversized, bamboo-laced, nest-inspired huts with outdoor showers. Try the 90-minute detoxifying organic-seaweed-leaf wrap. (☑076 358777; www.keemala. com; 10/88 Mu 6, Th Nakasud; massage 2900-5500B; ⏰9am-9pm)

Oasis Spa   SPA

4 MAP P102, C4

Dainty water features and a classic Thai setting welcome you at this excellent upper-midrange day spa, with branches across Thailand (including Kata and Ao Bang Thao). Tempting treatments include signature hot-oil massages, Ayurvedic massages, herbal clay wraps and body scrubs. Opt for a package

(from 2700B) to pick and choose. (☑076 337777; www.oasisspa.net; 128 Mu 3, Th Rim Hat; massage or treatment 1200-4600B; ⏰10am-10pm)

Eating

Blue Manao   THAI $$

5 MAP P102, B4

This relaxed, French-run eatery decked out in marine blue has more atmosphere than its nearby competitors, as well as a more individual menu. The seafood – barracuda, yellow-curry squid, grilled tiger prawns – is an obvious draw, but the traditional Thai curries (in meat, fish or vegetarian incarnations) are also excellent, as are the European desserts. It has a proper bar, too. (☑084 849 3830; 93/13 Mu 3, Th Rim Hat; mains 130-500B; ⏰12.30-11pm daily, closed Wed May-Aug, closed Sep; 🛜)

Taste Bar & Grill   INTERNATIONAL, THAI $$$

6 MAP P102, B4

Among colourful boards of chalked-up specials, this elegant terrace restaurant turns out fabulously fresh pizza-oven flatbreads garnished with delectable fusion toppings such as grilled aubergine with Thai basil and melted mozzarella, plus imaginative plates such as tamarind-glazed white snapper. Tapas-style bites roam from mushroom bruschetta to mango sticky rice. (☑087 886 6401; www. tastebargrill.com; Th Rim Hat; mains 290-590B; ⏰6am-late; 🛜🍽)

Isaan Popeye Thai Food THAI $

MAP P102, C4

One of the few restaurants in Kamala where you'll find locals dining, thanks to the winning combination of authentic and spicy northeastern dishes, fresh seafood and classic stir-fries and noodles, including omelette-wrapped *pàt tai*. This welcoming, straightforward spot also does Western-style breakfasts. It's 500m (a five-minute walk) inland from the beach. (74/43 Mu 3; mains 80-250B; ⏱9.30am-10pm; 🛜)

Meena Restaurant THAI $

8 MAP P102, C1

This welcoming, family-run beachside shack with sarongs for tablecloths is a real find. The fresh fruit shakes and authentic Thai food are exceptional, and the rustic setting is exactly why you came to Kamala. It's at the north end of the beach, but has moved around due to the beach clean-up – ask locally for the latest. (mains 80-150B; ⏱9am-5pm Nov-Apr)

Mam's Restaurant THAI, INTERNATIONAL $$

9 MAP P102, D4

There's no beach view, but local expats swear by this quiet, simple place with a handful of tables sprinkled across the patio of a family home. Mam's plates up Thai favourites (including excellent, vegetable-packed massaman curries), plus burgers, pastas, kebabs and even fish and chips. It's

400m east (inland) from the main highway. (☎089 032 2009; 32/32 Soi 8, Th Hua Khuan Tai; mains 100-350B; ⏱noon-10pm)

Mala Restaurant THAI, INTERNATIONAL $$$

The health-focused restaurant at ecofriendly, jungle-wrapped Keemala (see 3 Map p102, B6)) has an enormous menu of artfully presented Thai, Indian and international cooking, with ingredients sourced directly from its own gardens. Wood-carved walls, faux-faded mirrors and an elevated tree-house-feel setting create an elegant safari vibe. Charming service, good wines and imaginative dishes make it worth the 2km trip south from Kamala. (☎076 358777; www.keemala.com; 10/88 Mu 6, Th Nakasud; mains 300-800B; ⏱7am-10pm; 🅿🛜🍴)

Drinking

Café del Mar LOUNGE

10 MAP P102, C1

Ibiza's world-famous, original sunset-gazing brand brings its signature glam-chillout vibe to Phuket with this bold, distressed-concrete beach club on northern Hat Kamala. Umbrellas and day beds are strung around a gleaming pool; a multitiered terrace hosts DJ sessions and Sunday brunches (from 1860B). Cold-meats platters, tiger-prawn pastas and massaman curries mingle on the world-wandering menu (290B to 900B). (☎081 188 1230; www.cafedelmarphuket.com; 118/19 Mu 3; ⏱11am-2am)

Explore ⊛
Hat Surin

With a wide, blonde beach, water that blends from pale turquoise in the shallows to a deep blue on the horizon, and lush, boulder-strewn headlands, Surin (สุรินทร์) is one of Phuket's most attractive spots. It's very much (not exclusively) an upmarket destination, though Phuket's crackdown on unlicensed beachfront restaurants and bars has hit Surin particularly hard. For some, this is a blessing; others might find Surin a tad too peaceful.

The Short List

○ **Hat Surin & Hat Pansea (p109)** Wandering the golden expanses of these two gorgeous sandy sweeps, separated by a lush headland.

○ **Relax (p110)** There's little to do in Surin apart from laze by the pool, enjoy a massage and browse a few boutiques before heading out to dinner.

○ **Twin Palms Brunch (p110)** Getting into the glam-Phuket scene with Sunday brunch at this local favourite.

Getting There & Around

🚗 To/from airport 500B to 700B, Phuket Town 700B.

🚌 Phuket Smart Bus to/from airport (150B, hourly), west coast beaches and Rawai.

Sŏrng·tăa·ou To/from Phuket Town (40B) and Kamala (20B); 7am to 5pm.

Hat Surin Map on p108

Hat Pansea (p109) IMAGEBROKER/ALAMY STOCK PHOTO ©

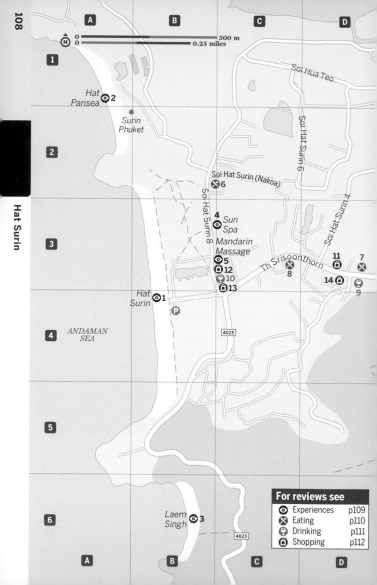

A	B	C	D

1

0   500 m
0   0.25 miles

Soi Hua Teo

Hat Pansea ⊙2

Surin Phuket

2

Soi Hat Surin 6

Soi Hat Surin (Nakoa)
✕6

Soi Hat Surin 8

3

4 Sun Spa
⊙
Mandarin Massage
⊙5
🏛12
Th Srisoonthorn
11 🔒
7 ✕
🍽10
🏛13
✕8
14 🔒
🍴9

Hat Surin ⊙1
🅿

4

ANDAMAN SEA

4025

5

6

Laem Singh ⊙3

4025

For reviews see	
⊙ Experiences	p109
✕ Eating	p110
🍽 Drinking	p111
🏛 Shopping	p112

A	B	C	D

Experiences

Hat Surin   BEACH

1 ⊙ MAP P108, B4

A beautiful sweep of blonde sand washed by Andaman waves, Hat Surin was particularly affected by the Phuket beach-clean-up operation, with all of its beach bars, clubs and restaurants forced to close or relocate. Despite this, Surin remains welcoming with a village vibe, and the near-empty beach is a welcome respite from Phuket's busier sands. (หาด สุรินทร์)

Hat Pansea   BEACH

2 ⊙ MAP P108, A1

Just north of Hat Surin, this exquisite little secluded strip of white-gold sand fringed by green-clad headlands is home to two exclusive resorts. Sunsets here are magical. (หาดพันซี)

Laem Singh   BEACH

3 ⊙ MAP P108, B6

Local beach addicts will tell you that cliff-framed Laem Singh, 1km south of Surin, conceals one of the island's most beautiful beaches. You usually park on the headland and clamber down a steep jungle-frilled path, but, at research time, the access trail was closed and

The Phuket Beach Clean-Up

Since 2014, there has been a crackdown on illegal construction and commercial activity on Phuket's overcrowded beaches.

Initially, all rental sunbeds, deckchairs and umbrellas were banned, with thousands removed under the watch of armed soldiers. Vendors, masseuses and restaurants on the sand were ordered off the beach. Illegally encroaching buildings were bulldozed, including well-established beach clubs and restaurants, and others dramatically reduced in size.

Some beaches have been affected more than others, and the positive side of the crackdown is that beaches are cleaner and less cluttered than before. Beach mats and umbrellas are still available to rent, in limited numbers and in allocated '10%' areas, and sunbeds returned to all beaches in 2017 (also within the '10%' allocated spaces). Tourists may pitch their own umbrellas and chairs within designated areas too. Of course, not everyone is abiding by the rules. Jet skis, which were suspended to begin with, are still very much operating in Patong, and some businesses have simply moved to new locations.

It's a confusing, fluid and typically Thai situation, so things may change again.

there are plans for a luxury hotel here. For now, boats run to Laem Singh from southern Hat Surin (return 100B per person, 400B for the whole boat). (แหลมสิงห์; **P**)

Sun Spa SPA

4 MAP P108, C3

Pamper yourself with a 'Travellers' Revival' facial, a white-clay body wrap, a Thai-herb bath and/or a signature Surin massage at this luxurious hotel-spa just back from the beach. It also offers mother-to-be massages and a full range of beauty services. The deluxe manicures and pedicures come highly recommended. (076 316500; www. twinpalms-phuket.com; Twin Palms, 106/46 Mu 3; massage or treatment 1500-3900B; 11am-8.30pm)

Mandarin Massage SPA

5 MAP P108, C3

A friendly, inexpensive massage parlour in clean, air-conditioned surrounds, with a short but sweet menu offering classic Thai massages and aloe-vera massages for those who've roasted themselves in the sun. (081 614 1204; 106/38 Mu 3; massage 500B; 10am-midnight)

Eating

Surin Chill House THAI, INTERNATIONAL $$

6 MAP P108, B2

Loved for its coffee, cakes and breakfasts (from fruit-salad bowls to omelettes and waffles), this relaxed, polished-concrete, cafe-like space does a bit of everything else too: spicy Thai curries and salads, seafood, fine pizza and some more challenging international mains. All the ingredients are fresh, the team is welcoming and it's very family-friendly. (076 636254; www.facebook.com/surin-chill-house-135990500200614; 107/3 Mu 3; mains 130-450B; 8.30am-4pm & 6-10pm Tue-Sun;)

Oriental Spoon THAI, INTERNATIONAL $$$

The sophisticated **Twin Palms resort** (d 8500-17,600B, ste 13,000-30,000B; **P** **@**) restaurant (see **4** Map p108, C3) gets lively for its popular Sunday brunch (1980B), but also serves elegantly prepared Thai and international fare, including an unusual selection of Peranakan dishes: a fusion of Thai, Chinese and Malay flavours, spicy and sour with lots of tamarind and lemongrass. There are tasty veggie and massaman curries, plus a comprehensive wine list. (076 316500; www. twinpalms-phuket.com; Twin Palms, 106/46 Mu 3; mains 290-1300B; 11am-11pm; **P**)

Bocconcino ITALIAN $$$

7 MAP P108, D3

An Italian deli may not be what you came to Phuket for, but Bocconcino's homemade gelato is classic Surin: refined and refreshing. This elegant, expat-frequented eatery houses an Italophile's dream of wines, coffee, cakes, cheeses, cured meats, homemade pastas, pizzas, panini and changing specials. Or try traditional salads such as tomato and mozzarella. It's 600m east of Hat Surin. (📞076 386532; www.bocconcinophuket.com; 8/71 Mu 3, Th Srisoonthorn; mains 300-500B; ⏰9am-10pm Aug-Apr, from 11.30am May-Jul; 🛜)

Blue Lagoon THAI $

8 MAP P108, C3

One of a dwindling number of Surin restaurants, following the crackdown on beachfront establishments, this friendly, family-run, semi-open-air joint serves up tasty versions of classic Thai dishes, from *sôm·dam* (spicy green-papaya salad) to curries and noodle soups, as

well as Western breakfasts. With check-cloth tables, swaying lanterns and a roadside terrace, it's more down-to-earth than most Surin eateries. (📞087 923 8235; Th Srisoonthorn; mains 120-200B; ⏰9am-11pm)

Drinking

Phuket Coffee Lab CAFE, COFFEE

9 MAP P108, D3

It's all about the freshly roasted, small-batch, single-origin Thai and international beans at this concrete-floored, industrial-feel cafe, 700m inland from Hat Surin. Skilled baristas deliver artisan coffees (65B to 120B) and professional training sessions, alongside enticing brunch-style bites (165B to 220B) roaming from smashed-

Hat Surin Drinking

Sôm·dam

Beach Bar

The low-key, pagoda-like **Beach Bar** (Map p106, A2; ☑076 316400; www.thesurinphuket.com; Surin Phuket, 118 Mu 3, Hat Pansea; ☺9am-midnight; ☜) at the swanky Surin Phuket has a glorious setting, perched on white sands at the southern end of beautiful Hat Pansea. It's a dreamy spot for sunset, when lanterns are lit and the horizon blazes in pinks and oranges. Cocktails (180B to 250B) are cheerfully tropical, and there are pre- and post-dinner happy hours.

avocado toast to courgette-and-feta omelette. (☑080 534 5512; www.facebook.com/phuketcoffeelab; 116/4 Mu 3, Th Srisoonthorn; ☺8am-4pm Tue-Sun; ☜)

9th Glass Wine Bar & Bistro
WINE BAR

10 🍸 MAP P108, C3

A sister venture to Patong's popular 9th Floor restaurant, this smart, intimate bar offers Surin's widest choice of wine, with 160 labels spanning Europe, Australia, New Zealand and South Africa, as well as properly mixed cocktails and a big liquor selection. Tapas, salads and Western-style mains (280B to 675B) help soak it all up. (www.the9thglass.com; 106/16 Mu 3; ☺4-10.30pm Mon-Sat)

Shopping

Chandra
FASHION & ACCESSORIES

11 🔒 MAP P108, D3

Fashionistas will adore this sparkly, sophisticated, Ko Samui–born boutique that captures all that's young and glam about Phuket. Flick through gorgeous, original breezy dresses, light kaftans, silk kimonos and bejewelled bikinis, designed in-house or sourced across Southeast Asia. Tones tend towards minimalist natural, with some bursts of colour. For men, there are linen shirts, silk-blend waistcoats and cotton tie-trousers. (☑076 621552; www.chandra-exotic.com; 8/44 Mu 3, Th Srisoonthorn; ☺10am-7pm Mon-Sat)

Lemongrass House
COSMETICS

12 🔒 MAP P108, C3

Phuket's top homegrown all-natural health and beauty producer, Lemongrass has shelves stacked high with moisturisers, body scrubs, essential oils, chunky soaps, tropical shampoos, lip balms and body washes – all infused with delicious exotic ingredients from jasmine, green tea, rose and papaya to its namesake lemongrass. The nontoxic lavender-and-citronella mosquito repellent really does the job. (☑076 325501; www.lemongrasshousethailand.com; 106/13 Mu 3; ☺9am-8pm)

Hat Surin (p109)

Oriental Fine Art

ANTIQUES, ART

13 🔒 MAP P108, C3

One of the best collections of traditional Southeast Asian art in Thailand, this multilevel, museum-quality showroom displays a 3m Buddha encrusted with precious stones, an ancient teak shrine, terracotta sculptures, wooden Chinese furniture and other antique surprises. Absolutely everything is for sale. (☏076 271144; heritage99@hotmail.com; 106/19-20 Mu 3; ☺10am-7pm)

Soul of Asia

ART

14 🔒 MAP P108, D3

A beautiful gallery filled with fine Southeast Asian and Chinese modern and traditional art, mixed with a few antiques and original prints and lithographs from art masters such as Picasso, Miró and Warhol. (☏076 271629; www.soulofasia.com; Surin Plaza, 5/50 Mu 3, Th Srisoonthorn; ☺10.30am-7pm Mon-Sat, 2-6pm Sun)

Explore
Ao Bang Thao & Cherngtalay

A sweeping 8km of dusty white sand, Hat Bang Thao (หาดบางเทา) is the glue binding together northwestern Phuket's buzzy Cherngtalay (เชิงทะเล) district. The region's southern end is dotted with midrange resorts and beach clubs; smack in the centre of it all is the Laguna Phuket complex. Inland you'll find an old, canal-laced, largely Muslim fishing village, plus some stellar restaurants. At the northern end of Ao Bang Thao (อ่าวบางเทา), mother nature reasserts herself, and powdery sands extend into peaceful bliss.

The Short List

○ **Beaches (p117)** Kicking back on Phuket's most glorious beaches, at its chicest beach clubs.

○ **Dining Delights (p118)** Diving into some of Phuket's finest international cuisine.

○ **Soul-soothing spas (p117)** From cheap-and-cheerful parlours to five-star sensations.

Getting There & Around

🚗 To/from airport 700B, southwest beaches 900B.

🚌 Phuket Smart Bus to/from airport (100B, hourly), west coast beaches and Rawai.

Sŏrng·tăa·ou & *túk-túk* Passenger pick-up trucks to/from Phuket Town (35B, 7am to 5pm); túk-túk 450B.

Ao Bang Thao & Cherngtalay Map on p116

Banyan Tree Spa resort (p117) MICHAEL SNELL/ALAMY STOCK PHOTO ©

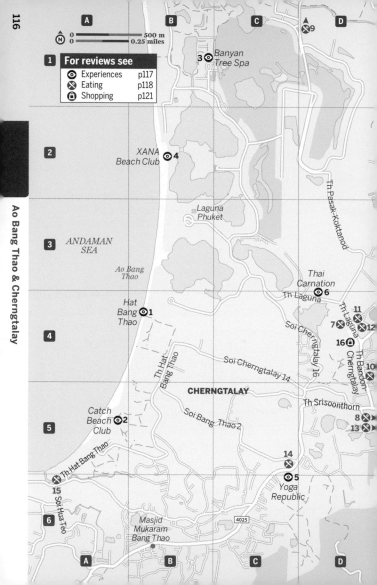

For reviews see
- ⊙ Experiences p117
- ✕ Eating p118
- 🔒 Shopping p121

0 — 500 m
0 — 0.25 miles

Banyan Tree Spa **3** ⊙

XANA Beach Club ⊙ **4**

Laguna Phuket

ANDAMAN SEA

Ao Bang Thao

Thai Carnation ⊙ **6**
Th Laguna

Hat Bang Thao ⊙ **1**

Soi Cherngtalay 16

7 ✕ 11 ✕
        12

16 🔒

Th Laguna

Th Bandon Cherngtalay

10 ✕

Soi Cherngtalay 14

Th Hat Bang Thao

CHERNGTALAY

Th Srisoonthorn

Catch Beach Club ⊙ **2**

Soi Bang Thao 2

8 ✕
13 ✕

Th Hat Bang Thao

14 ✕

⊙ **5**
Yoga Republic

15 ✕

Soi Hua Teo

Masjid Mukaram Bang Thao

4025

✕ 9

Th Pasak-Koktanod

Experiences

Hat Bang Thao   BEACH

1  MAP P116, B4

Beautiful 8km-long Hat Bang Thao is one of the longest, dreamiest beaches on Phuket. This slice of sand is just asking for you to laze around on it, with midrange bungalows at the south end and luxury resorts in the middle. A couple of beach clubs now dot its southern and northern tips. (หาดบางเทา)

Catch Beach Club   BEACH CLUB

2 MAP P116, A5

There's a day at the beach, and then there's a day at Catch – arguably Phuket's most fashionable beach club (now relocated from Surin to southern Hat Bang Thao). Slip into

your chicest beachwear for party-vibe lazing overlooking white sands and perfect blue waters. Day passes include towels and outdoor showers plus food and drink. The beachfront bar-restaurant (p119) buzzes until late. (📞 065 348 2017; www.catch beachclub.com; 202/88 Mu 2, Hat Bang Thao; day pass 2000B; 🕘9am-late)

Banyan Tree Spa   SPA

3 MAP P116, B1

At this highly regarded luxury-resort spa, choose from a wide selection of Indian- and Thai-inspired treatments, fruit-and-spice scrubs (how about a honey-turmeric cleanser?) and traditional Thai massages. There are also calming detox baths, soothing facials and couples' packages. Or just book in for the whole day. By advance

Catch Beach Club

Masjid Mukaram Bang Thao

The busy mosque **Masjid Mukaram Bang Thao** (มัสยิด มุการ์มบางเทา; Map p116, B6; Rte 4025; admission free; ☉daylight hours) provides a good insight into Phuket village life and makes an interesting change of scene from the beach. The cream-coloured facade and sea-green mosaic domes loom strikingly against the blue sky and jungly hills, and it's home to a friendly Muslim congregation who set up tasty halal street-food carts outside. Visitors welcome.

appointment only. (☏076 372400; www.banyantreespa.com; Laguna Phuket, 33/27 Mu 4, Th Srisoonthorn; massage or treatment 3000-10,000B; ☉10am-10pm)

XANA Beach Club
BEACH CLUB

4 ◉ MAP P116, B2

Catering to a fashionable, fun-loving crowd, Phuket's beachfront outpost of Singaporean club brand Attica stands on a fabulous swathe of silky white sand, halfway along Hat Bang Thao. Come for the polished red-on-white decor, the raised 35m pool with swim-up bar, eight-person cabanas and in-water sunbeds, the 'Sunday Fun Brunch', a pumping sound system and international-DJ sets. Check online for upcoming events. (☏076 358500; www. xanabeachclub.com; Angsana Laguna Phuket, 10 Mu 4, Th Srisoonthorn, Hat Bang Thao; ☉10am-midnight, reduced hours May-Oct)

Yoga Republic
YOGA

5 ◉ MAP P116, C6

A stylish, contemporary studio, complete with juice bar, that hosts an excellent line-up of drop-in yoga sessions to suit all levels, from 'hot yang' to 'fusion flow', along with teacher-training courses. It's led by experienced yogi Jack Farras and sits on Rte 4025, 2km east from southern Hat Bang Thao. Check class schedules online. (☏082 280 3914; www.yogarepublic.co; 123/3-5 Mu 5, Th Srisoonthorn; class 550B; ☉9am-8pm)

Thai Carnation
SPA

6 ◉ MAP P116, D4

Impressively professional yet wonderfully low-key, this fantastic-value spa is a real find, with private massage rooms, well-trained therapists and a local vibe. Ease away tensions with a classic Thai massage, an Indian head massage or an exfoliating Asian-glow scrub. It's 1.5km east from Hat Bang Thao. (☏076 325565; www.thai-carnation.com; 64 Th Laguna; massage or treatment 500-1400B; ☉11am-10.30pm)

Eating

Bampot
INTERNATIONAL $$$

7 ✖ MAP P116, D4

Cool-blue booths, an open-plan kitchen and white-brick walls plastered with artwork set the scene for chef Jamie Wakeford's ambitious, contemporary European-inspired cooking – cashew-pesto risotto, crispy-skinned salmon with braised fennel, cauliflower tempura drizzled with truffle mayo. Throw in expertly crafted cocktails (try a gin-based BGT), excellent wines and cheerfully professional service, and Bampot delivers as one of Phuket's top international restaurants. (093 586 9828; www.bampot.co; 19/1 Mu 1, Th Laguna; mains 550-1200B; 6pm-midnight, closed Mon May-Nov;)

Suay
FUSION, THAI $$$

8 MAP P116, D5

Launched in 2017 in a sleek glassed-in space, the Cherngtalay branch of star Phuket chef Noi Tammasak's sought-after Suay is a fusion-tastic sensation. Menus feature such creative delights as mushroom carpaccio, lemongrass-grilled lamb chops, Shanghai noodles dressed in sweet-basil pesto and tofu steak doused in *kôw soy* sauce. Don't miss the reimagined mango sticky rice with sesame ice cream. (093 339 1890; www.suayrestaurant.com; 177/99 Wana Park, Mu 4, Th Srisoonthorn; mains 350-650B; 4-11pm; P)

Project Artisan
INTERNATIONAL, THAI $$$

9 MAP P116, D1

Peachy-pink and pineapple-yellow wood-carved doors frame a lantern-lit garden adorned with dreamcatchers at this boho-chic, Bali-inspired, multipurpose creative venue in northern Cherngtalay. Locally sourced breakfasts of just-baked pastries, tropical smoothie bowls, artisan sliders and organic Phang-Nga eggs are followed by live-music sessions, massages at Saparod Spa (900B to 1800B), and cocktails or Thai craft beers at street-food-stall-style Tipsy Bar. (093 790 9911; www.theprojectartisan.com; 53/17 Mu 6, Rte 4018; meals 200-600B; 8.30am-11pm; P)

Pesto
THAI, INTERNATIONAL $$

10 MAP P116, D4

Mix a Paris-trained Thai chef with a simple street-side, semi-open-air setting and you get delicious, wallet-friendly Thai and international food. Sweet-basil-pesto penne and prawn tagliatelle hint at the Mediterranean, or stay local with salmon steak on green-mango salad, *dôm yam gûng* (spicy-sour prawn soup), deep-fried fish of the day and all your favourite curries. (082 423 0184; Th Bandon-Cherngtalay; mains 140-500B; 11.30am-11pm Sun-Fri, from 5pm Sat;)

Catch Beach Club
INTERNATIONAL, THAI $$$

Throw on your breeziest island-chic outfit to dine by the sand at Bang Thao's (and, arguably, Phuket's) glitziest beach club (see 2 Map p116, A5). There's a mellow-party atmosphere and the beachfront setting is divine, while the

Dining at Anantara Phuket Layan

On its own secluded, wild-feel bay just north of Hat Bang Thao, the exquisite **Anantara Phuket Layan** (076 317200; www.anantara.com; 168 Mu 6, Soi 4, Hat Layan; incl breakfast d 10,140-15,780B, one-bedroom villa 11,820-38,450B; P ❄ 🛜 ⛱) hosts a chic, laid-back lounge-bar overlooking a beachside pool, as well as three excellent restaurants; you can even dine at a private lantern-lit beach table.

Thai-international dishes wander from perfectly spiced *pàt tai* and juicy tuna steak to vegan coconut curry, whole-roasted snapper, crab-meat pasta and succulent Wagyu tenderloin. (065 348 2017; www.catchbeachclub.com; 202/88 Mu 2, Hat Bang Thao; mains 390-1390B; ⏰11am-11am; P 🛜 🍴)

Siam Supper Club INTERNATIONAL $$$

11 MAP P116, D4

One of Cherngtalay's swishest spots, with a dressed-up, dimly lit, old-school atmosphere, the Supper Club is all about sipping signature cocktails to a soothing soundtrack of jazz and 1950s-style lounge music. The menu is predominantly international: gourmet pizzas, hearty steaks, seafood dishes, tasty pastas and an impressive wine list. Monday night jazz (8pm to 11pm) is hugely popular; book ahead. (076 270936; www.siamsupperclub.com; 36-40 Th Laguna; mains 290-1390B; ⏰6pm-1am; 🛜 🍴)

Tatonka INTERNATIONAL, FUSION $$$

12 MAP P116, D4

Well-established, cheerful and welcoming, Tatonka bills itself as the home of 'globetrotter cuisine', which owner-chef Harold Schwarz has developed by blending local products with cooking techniques learned in Europe, Colorado and Hawaii. The inventive world-roaming selection includes such delights as tuna tacos, green-curry pasta, Thai bouillabaisse and mushroom-stuffed rice-paper rolls. Dine among lanterns in a courtyard wrapped in greenery. (076 324349; www.facebook.com/tatonkaphuket; 34 Th Laguna; mains 350-550B; ⏰6-10pm Mon-Sat; 🛜 🍴)

Gallery Cafe CAFE $$

13 MAP P116, D5

Fresh in 2018, the minimalist-chic Cherngtalay outpost of Pinky's beloved Phuket Town–born cafe-restaurant hits the all-day-breakfast spot with spinach-stuffed omelettes, colourful smoothie bowls, home-baked breads and bagels, and smashed avo with feta. Coffees arrive on wooden trays with bite-sized cake chunks, or try a mango-passionfruit smoothie. It's a stylish hang-around-all-day lounge: concrete floors, communal tables, shiplike windows and a sunny terrace. (089 103 7000;

www.gallerycafephuket.com; 122/4 Th Srisoonthorn; meals 140-350B; ⏱8am-8pm; (P 🛜 🖊 👪)

Taste Bar & Grill   INTERNATIONAL, FUSION $$$

14 ❌ MAP P116, C5

Minimalist modern lines, a sophisticated but chilled-out vibe and a deliciously inventive fusion menu inspired by Thai and Mediterranean flavours make Taste a favourite Bang Thao address. The steaks, topped flatbreads and Nepalese-style vegetable curry are excellent, as are the enormous crispy-fresh salads and original starters (from fried Camembert to spicy coconut-grilled squid), and there's a good wine list. (📞087 886 6401; www.taste bargrill.com; 3/2 Mu 5, Th Srisoonthorn; mains 390-990B; ⏱3pm-midnight Wed-Mon; 🛜)

Nok & Jo's   THAI, INTERNATIONAL $$

15 ❌ MAP P116, A6

On a quiet road at the southern end of Ao Bang Thao, this ramshackle, ranch-like, Canadian-Thai-owned sports bar and restaurant serves an extensive Thai-international menu. Varnished driftwood furniture mingles with globe-roaming flags, number plates

and boating paraphernalia. There are cooking classes (2000B), a fun *gà·teu·i* (also *kàthoey;* Thai transgender and cross dressers) cabaret on Wednesdays and barbecue buffets on Saturdays (499B). (📞081 538 2110; www.facebook.com/Nok-Jos-Famous-Restaurant-Bangtao-150777748318923; 37/1 Mu 3, Hat Bang Thao; mains 100-500B; ⏱noon-late; 🛜)

Shopping

Boat Avenue   FASHION & ACCESSORIES

16 🔒 MAP P116, D4

Partly set in colourfully reincarnated shipping containers, this upmarket open-air shopping centre hosts an array of beach-chic, glam-Phuket fashion boutiques – **Chandra** (www.chandra-exotic.com; Boat Avenue, 49/14 Th Bandon-Cherngtalay; ⏱10am-8pm, closed Sun Jun-Aug) and **Wings by hejselbjerg** (www.facebook.com/Hejselbjerg; Boat Avenue, 49/14 Th Bandon-Cherngtalay; ⏱9am-9pm) are standouts – as well as cafes, bars, a fitness studio and a popular Friday **night market** (Boat Avenue, 49/14 Th Bandon-Cherngtalay; meals 50-100B; ⏱4pm-late Fri). (49/14 Th Bandon-Cherngtalay; ⏱10am-6pm, hours vary)

Explore
Northeastern Phuket

Phuket's lush northeastern region is laced with waterfalls, temples, singing gibbons and jungle-wreathed hills. Untouristed Thalang (ถลาง) unfolds around the Heroines Monument, 13km north of Phuket Town; there are some intriguing cultural attractions to be unearthed here. But most visitors swing through Thalang en route to the northeast's two very worthwhile conservation operations.

The Short List

○ **Phuket Elephant Sanctuary (p127)** Meeting magnificent pachyderms at the island's only genuine refuge.

○ **Phuket Gibbon Rehabilitation Project (p125)** Learning about Thai gibbons at this volunteer run project.

○ **Khao Phra Thaew Royal Wildlife & Forest Reserve (p126)** Hiking to luscious waterfalls.

○ **Temples (p125)** Uncovering Phuket's Buddhist heritage.

Getting There & Around

🚗 Phuket Town/west-coast beaches to Phuket Elephant Sanctuary around 700B/800B.

Sŏrng·tăa·ou Passenger pick-up trucks from Phuket Town to Surin and Ao Bang Thao pass by the Heroines Monument (30B, 7am to 5pm).

Northeastern Phuket Map on p124

Phuket Elephant Sanctuary (p127) GINA SMITH/SHUTTERSTOCK ©

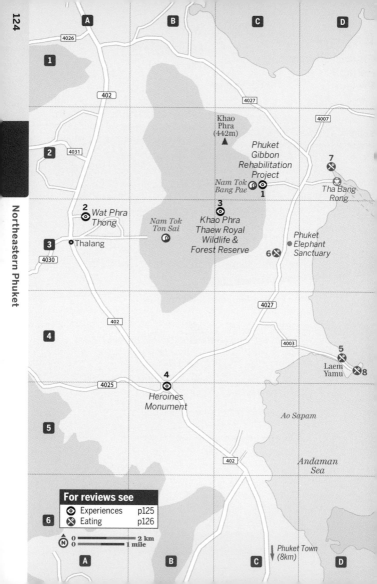

For reviews see

◉ Experiences   p125
✖ Eating   p126

Experiences

Phuket Gibbon Rehabilitation Project

WILDLIFE RESERVE

1 ⊙ MAP P124, C2

Financed by donations (2100B sponsors a gibbon for a year), this tiny sanctuary adopts gibbons previously kept in captivity in the hope of reintroducing them to the wild. You can meet the gibbons on low-key visits; swing by around 9am to hear their morning song. You can't get too close to the animals, but the volunteer work here is outstanding. (โครงการคืนชะนีสู่ป่า; ☎076 260492; www.gibbonproject.org; off Rte 4027; admission by donation; ⊙9am-4.30pm Sun-Fri, to 3pm Sat; P)

Wat Phra Thong

BUDDHIST TEMPLE

2 ⊙ MAP P124, A3

About 7km north of the Heroines Monument (p126), Phuket's tranquil, 250-year-old 'Temple of the Golden Buddha' revolves around a half-buried statue, with only the head and shoulders visible. According to legend, the image simply emerged from the ground, and those who have tried to excavate it have become ill or encountered serious accidents. The temple is particularly revered by Thai-Chinese, who believe the image hails from China. During Chinese New Year, pilgrims descend from Phang-Nga, Takua Pa and Krabi. (วัดพระทอง; off Hwy 402; admission free; ⊙daylight hours; P)

Wat Phra Thong

Khao Phra Thaew Royal Wildlife & Forest Reserve
WILDLIFE RESERVE

3 ⊙ MAP P124, C3

On the north half of the island, this lush reserve protects 23 sq km of virgin island rainforest (evergreen monsoon forest). Because of its royal status, it's better protected than the average national park in Thailand. Tigers, Malayan sun bears, rhinos and elephants once roamed the forest here, but nowadays resident animals are limited to wild boars, monkeys, slow loris, langurs, gibbons, civets, flying foxes, cobras, pythons, squirrels and other smaller creatures. The reserve's highest point is Khao Phra (442m).

There are pleasant hill hikes and some photogenic waterfalls, including Nam Tok Ton Sai (accessed from the west off Hwy 402, 6km northwest of the Heroines Monument) and **Nam Tok Bang Pae** (น้ำตกบางแป; off Rte 4027; adult/child 200/100B; ⊙9am-5pm). The falls are most impressive during the June-to-November monsoon; an 8km walking trail runs between the two (you'll probably need a park guide). Park rangers may guide hikers on request (around 1500B); ask at park access points. (อุทยานสัตว์ป่าเขา พระแทว; off Rte 4027 & Hwy 402; adult/ child 200/100B; ⊙9am-5pm)

Heroines Monument
MONUMENT

4 ⊙ MAP P124, B5

Phuket's 'two heroines', Chan and Mook, supposedly drove off an 18th-century Burmese invasion by convincing the island's women to dress like male soldiers; the sisters are immortalised, swords in hand, on a hectic roundabout at the near-centre of the island. (อนุสาวรีย์ท้าวเทพ กษัตรีท้าวศรีสุนทร; Hwy 402)

Eating

Breeze
INTERNATIONAL $$$

5 ✖ MAP P124, D4

Elegant yet understated, one of Phuket's finest restaurants sits in glorious hilltop, sea-surrounded seclusion, 20km northeast of Phuket Town. Blue beanbags overlook the pool and sea from the pillared open-walled dining hall. The divine, inventive European-style dishes are infused with local, often-home-grown produce. Menus change regularly. Classic cocktails are given a Thai twist. Book ahead. (☎081 271 2320; www.breezecapeyamu.com; 224 Mu 7, Laem Yamu; mains 750-1600B, 5-course tasting menus 2000B; ⊙noon-10pm Wed-Sun; P 🛜 🌶)

Monkeypod
CAFE $$

6 ✖ MAP P124, C3

A striking minimalist-white creation with floor-to-ceiling windows and a leafy outlook, this contemporary family-run cafe is a welcome surprise close to the Phuket Elephant Sanctuary and Phuket Gibbon Rehabilitation Project (p125). The coffee, smoothies and home-cooked food are all delicious, with reasonably priced salads, pastas, wraps and cakes served alongside

Phuket Elephant Sanctuary

The island's only genuine elephant refuge, the **Phuket Elephant Sanctuary** (Map p122, C3; ☏088 752 3853; www.phuketelephantsanctuary. org; 100 Mu 2, Paklok, Rte 4027; adult/child 3000/1500B; ☉9.30am-1pm & 2-5.30pm; ▮) protects aged pachyderms who were mistreated for decades while working in logging and tourism. During the morning tour, you get to feed them, before tagging along a few metres away as they wander the forest, chomp on watermelons, bathe and hang out. It's a rare, environmentally responsible opportunity that visitors rave about.

The sanctuary is a sister project to Chiang Mai's respected Elephant Nature Park and home to eight female elephants. There's no public access except via a tour, which must be booked in advance. The sanctuary picks up visitors from its nearby office; you'll be dropped back there afterwards. Less-interactive afternoon tours involve observing the elephants on a safari-like experience. Beware copycat 'sanctuaries' and taxi drivers on commission to take you elsewhere. The sanctuary accepts volunteers for one, three or seven days; fees (4500B, 8000B or 16,000B respectively) go towards elephant care.

Phuketian classics. It's 6km north-east of the Heroines Monument. (☏087 909 5252; www.facebook.com/monkeypodcoffeehouse; Rte 4027; mains 140-200B; ☉8.30am-8.30pm Tue-Sun; 🕸🌱)

Bang Rong Seafood

THAI, SEAFOOD $$

7 ✗ MAP P124, D2

This rustic fish farm turned restaurant sits on a floating pier, reached via a wooden boardwalk from Bang Rong pier. Your catch – red and white snapper, crab or mussels – is plucked after you order; you can have everything steamed, fried, grilled, boiled or baked. It also has classic stir-fries. This is a Muslim enterprise, so there's no beer. (☏089 872 4394; Tha Bang Rong, off Rte 4027; mains 120-350B; ☉10am-6pm)

La Sirena

ITALIAN $$$

8 ✗ MAP P124, D4

Perched by a pale-aqua infinity pool at Point Yamu by Como (p146), this contemporary southern-Italian restaurant makes the most of its sea views across Ao Phang-Nga's karst islets, with a sweeping terrace, turquoise-sprinkled decor and floor-to-ceiling windows. Beautifully executed dishes, some with local inspiration, include blue-crab linguini, wood-fired pizzas and roast-vegetable ciabatta sandwiches, along with some Thai favourites. (☏076 360100; www.comohotels.com; 225 Mu 7, Paklok, Laem Yamu; mains 430-750B; ☉8am-11pm; 🅿🕸🌱)

Explore ◈

Northern Beaches

Phuket's northwest coast is one of its sweetest slices: if you're chasing what remains of the island's beach seclusion and tranquillity, where nature and tourism still (just about) manage to coexist, this is it. Within a 15-minute drive of the airport lie some of Phuket's dreamiest and least-developed beaches: easygoing Hat Nai Thon, fun-loving Hat Nai Yang and magnificent, 10km-long Hat Mai Khao; all three are protected by Sirinat National Park. Kitesurfers flock to Nai Yang from May to October.

The Short List

○ **Beaches (p131)** Enjoying the three gorgeous white sweeps of sand protected by Sirinat National Park.

○ **Kitesurfing (p133)** Skimming the waves off Hat Nai Yang during the monsoon.

○ **Black Ginger (p133)** Arriving aboard a hand-pulled barge for an exquisite Thai dinner.

○ **Massage Mania (p132)** Indulging in a spa session or two at this area's swish resorts.

Getting There & Around

🚗 Around 300B to 600B to/from the airport, 900B to/from Patong and 800B to 1000B to/from Phuket Town.

Northern Beaches Map on p130

Hat Nai Yang (p131) BENNYARTIST/SHUTTERSTOCK ©

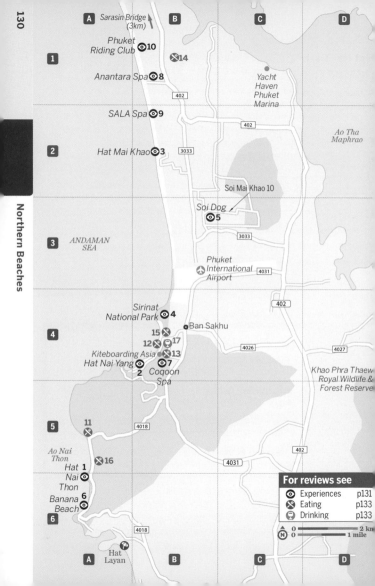

Experiences

Hat Nai Thon   BEACH

1 ⊙ MAP P130, A6

A lovely protected strip of fine, golden west-coast sand fringed by jungle, 7km south of the airport and blissfully removed from Phuket's busy buzz. Swimming is good (except at the height of the monsoon) and Nai Thon's blazing pink-orange sunsets are something to remember. (หาดในทอน)

Hat Nai Yang   BEACH

2 ⊙ MAP P130, B4

The liveliest and most developed of Phuket's three relaxed northern national-park beaches, this sandy blonde casuarina-shaded bay, 3km south of the airport, is sheltered by

a reef that slopes 20m below the surface – which means good snorkelling in high season and fantastic kitesurfing during the monsoon. Behind is a strip of seafood restaurants, hotels and mellow bars. (หาดในยาง)

Hat Mai Khao   BEACH

3 ⊙ MAP P130, B2

Dotted with a few upmarket resorts, Phuket's longest beach is a beautiful, secluded 10km stretch of pearl-white national-park sand extending from just south of the airport to the island's northernmost point. Except on weekends and Thai holidays, you'll mostly have it to yourself. Sea turtles lay eggs here between November and February. Take care with the strong year-round undertow (หาดไม้ขาว)

Hat Nai Thon

Northern Beaches Experiences

Sirinat National Park
NATIONAL PARK

4 MAP P130, B4

Comprising the exceptional northwestern beaches of Nai Thon (p131), Nai Yang (p131) and Mai Khao (p131), as well as the former Nai Yang National Park and Mai Khao Wildlife Reserve, Sirinat National Park encompasses 22 sq km of coastal land, plus 68 sq km of sea, stretching from the northern reaches of Ao Bang Thao to the northernmost tip of the island. Park headquarters, with **accommodation** (camping per person 30B, bungalows 700-1000B; P ❄), a basic visitors centre and a restaurant, are at the northern end of Hat Nai Yang. (อุทยานแห่งชาติสิรินาถ; ☎076 327152, 076 328226; www.portal.dnp.go.th; 89/1 Mu 1, Hat Nai Yang; adult/child 200/100B; ☉6am-6pm)

Soi Dog
VOLUNTEERING

5 MAP P130, B3

This nonprofit foundation protects hundreds of cats and dogs (many rescued from the illegal dog-meat trade), focusing on sterilisation, castration, rehoming and animal-welfare awareness. Visits are by in-depth tour. The 'old dogs' enclosure can be upsetting, but it's a happy home. Visitors can play with the animals, or become dog-walking, long-term or animal-transfer volunteers. (Gill Daley Foundation; ☎076 681029; www.soidog.org; 167/9 Mu 4, Soi Mai Khao 10; admission by donation; ☉9am-noon & 1-3.30pm Mon-Fri, 9am-noon Sat, tours 9.30am, 11am, 1.30pm & 2.30pm Mon-Fri, 9.30am & 11am Sat)

Banana Beach
BEACH

6 MAP P130, A6

Though not quite the secret it once was, this silky little tucked-away beach, 2km south of Hat Nai Thon, makes a refreshingly rustic Phuket escape. From a tiny parking space on the west side of the winding coastal Rte 4018, you clamber down through a jungle of coconut palms to beautifully quiet sands sprinkled with boulders and a single restaurant. (Hat Hin Gluai; หาดหินกล้วย; off Rte 4018)

Coqoon Spa
SPA

7 MAP P130, B4

Set within the uberstylish **Slate resort** (incl breakfast d 8200-24,300B villas 44,900-62,000B; P ❄ 🛜 🏊), which doubles as a monument to Phuket's tin-mining past, this is a fantastic, unique spa where treatment rooms are backed by lush gardens. Therapies include purple-frangipani scrubs, bamboo-charcoal wraps, Anne Semonin facials and detoxes in a suspended 'nest' suite. Book ahead. (☎076 327006; www.theslatephuket.com; Slate, 116 Mu 1, Hat Nai Yang; massage or treatment 2200-7000B; ☉10am-8pm)

Anantara Spa
SPA

8 MAP P130, B1

Escape into a tranquil, elegant oasis of lotus-filled ponds, timber boardwalks and couples' treatment rooms at this luxury spa within the **Anantara Phuket** (d incl breakfast 1,800-50,000B; P ❄ @ 🤗 ≈) resort. Tropical-oriented treatments include green-tea scrubs, after-sun wraps, Ayurvedic head massages and full-day rituals. Reservations recommended. (☎076 336100; www.phuket.anantara.com; Anantara Phuket, 888 Mu 3, Hat Mai Khao; massage or treatment 3500-6500B; ⏰10am-10pm)

SALA Spa   SPA

🔵 MAP P130, B2

Enjoy your classic Thai massage or soothing water-lily body wrap at this sexy yet graceful Sino-Portuguese-inspired spa **resort** (d incl breakfast 7500-29,000B; P ❄ 🤗 ≈), where treatments happen on beachfront cabanas or in peaceful private pods with tubs gracing pebbled courtyards. It's the kind of place that makes you feel fabulous just by being there. Bookings advised. (☎076 338888; www.salahospitality.com; SALA Phuket, 333 Mu 3, Hat Mai Khao; massage or treatment 1900-4900B; ⏰10am-10pm)

Phuket Riding Club   HORSE RIDING

🔵 MAP P130, B1

The perfect opportunity to live out that horse-riding-through-the-tropics dream, this long-running outfit offers fun one- or two-hour rides along the beaches and interior of northern Phuket. Book a day ahead. (☎081 787 2455; www.phuketridingclub.com; 60/9 Th Thepasattri, Mu 3, Mai Khao; 1/2hr rides 1200/2200B; ⏰8am-6.30pm)

Kitesurfing on Hat Nai Yang

During the May-to-October monsoon, Hat Nai Yang is great for kitesurfing. A number of schools, including **Kiteboarding Asia** (Map p128, B4; p93) and Rawai-based **Kite Zone**, teach budding kitesurfers.

Eating & Drinking

Black Ginger   THAI $$$

Reached only by hand-pulled barge, this lagoon-side restaurant is a magical spot (see 7 🔵 Map p130, B4), with traditional-style wood-walled *săh·lah* (pavilions; often spelt *sala*) and sparkling fire-lit lanterns. The sophisticated all-Thai menu, with many veggie versions available, has a strong focus on southern-Thai classics, like stir-fried *pàk miang* (kale-like leaves, often scrambled with eggs) and crab-meat curry served on rice noodles. Don't miss the beautiful cashew-nut ice cream. (☎076 327006; www.theslatephuket.com; Slate, 116 Mu 1, Hat Nai Yang; mains 280-675B; ⏰6-11pm; P 🤗 🍴)

Elements   INTERNATIONAL, THAI $$$

11 🍽 MAP P130, A5

Perched on the cliffs at the northern end of the beach, Nai Thon's glitziest **resort** (d 6000-12,000B, villas 29,000-32,000B; P ❄ @ 🤗 ≈) offers sophisticated Thai-international food in a swish indoor-outdoor dining room with thick pillars, abstract modern art and beautiful views across the bay. Service is friendly yet professional and on Fridays the restaurant fires up a seafood barbecue. (☑ 076 303299; www.pullmanphuketarcadia.com; Pullman, 22/2 Mu 4, Hat Nai Thon; mains 300-1300B; ⊙ noon-10.30pm; 🛜)

Phen's Restaurant
THAI, SEAFOOD $$

12 🍴 MAP P130, B4

Turquoise-on-white tablecloths and attentive staff make Phen's a popular beachside choice. It's one of just a few Phuket spots where you can still dine with sand between your toes. Expect masses of barbecued fresh seafood (lemon-fried crab, red-curry snapper, chilli-smoked shrimp), as well as Phuket favourites such as coconut *pàk miang* and *gaang som pla* (southern-style fish curry). (☑ 081 895 9489; www.facebook.com/phensrestaurant; Hat Nai Yang; mains 130-450B; ⊙ 10am-11pm; 🛜)

Mr Kobi
THAI $$

13 🍴 MAP P130, B4

The signs say 'Broken English spoken here perfect', but the ever-popular Mr Kobi speaks English very well. He handles the drinks, while Malee deals with the seafood and Thai faves served up in refreshingly unpretentious surroundings decorated with international flags. One wall is dedicated to the story of the 2004 tsunami. (Hat Nai Yang; mains 180-300B; ⊙ 10am-11pm)

Kin Dee
THAI $$

14 🍴 MAP P130, B1

For a change from Mai Khao's upmarket offerings, seek out this charming, low-key Thai-food specialist, set in a semi-open red-brick pavilion with dangling plants, 400m east off Hwy 402. Thoughtfully prepared dishes use local produce, and you can eat at riverside tables. It's signposted 3km south of the Sarasin Bridge (U-turn required). (☑ 082 814 8482; www.kindeerestaurant.com; 71/6 Mu 5, Mai Khao; mains 150-590B; ⊙ 11am-10pm; 🛜)

Aleta
INTERNATIONAL, THAI $$$

15 🍴 MAP P130, B4

Swing by Nai Yang's boutique-inspired **Cachet Resort Dewa Phuket** (incl breakfast d 3800-10,000B; villas 8500-14,400B; 🅿 ❄ 🛜 ⛱) for upscale Thai/international fare in a classy setting overlooking a lovely pool and a chill-out bar strewn with bean-bags. It's particularly hot on freshly grilled meats and seafood, such as burgers, lamb cutlets and banana-leaf sea bass, but also packs in plenty of pastas, pizzas, risottos and Thai curries and stir-fries. (☑ 076 372300; www.cachethotels.com; Cachet Resort Dewa Phuket, 65 Mu 1, Hat Nai Yang; meals 250-600B; ⊙ 11am-10.30pm; 🛜)

Coconut Tree
THAI $$

16 🍴 MAP P130, A5

This relaxed spot towards the south end of Hat Nai Thon rustles up quality seafood dishes such as stir-fried crab with black pepper, tiger prawns cooked in everything from yellow curry to bitter ginger, and curries, noodles and stir-fries, on a rustic semi-open veranda with a few pot plants. The Andaman sparkles across the road beyond soaring palms and casuarinas. (Rte 4018, Hat Nai Thon; mains 100-500B; ⊙10am-10pm; 🛜)

Stonehaus CAFE $$

Pocketed away in the Cachet Resort Dewa Phuket (see 15 ✕ Map p130, B4), across the road from Hat Nai Yang, this smart, small cafe and wine bar is a decent spot for your morning espresso or something stronger later on. It does an all-day breakfast (290B) along with cold cuts, cheese boards and fresh sandwiches and pastries. (📞076 372300; www.cachet-hotels.com; Cachet Resort Dewa Phuket, 65 Mu 1, Hat Nai Yang; snacks 30-290B; ⊙8am-6pm; 🛜)

NY Beach Republic LOUNGE

17 🚇 MAP P130, B4

As nightlifey as Nai Yang gets, this stylish, palm-studded, sandy-floored lounge bar and restaurant sits just back from the beach, sprinkled with bamboo booths, tall wooden tables, nautical-striped cushions and a snooker table. The bar serves fruity Chalong Bay rum mojitos (250B) and beers jugs (200B); the Thai menu (150B to 450B) is packed with seafood, soups, noodles and curries. (www.facebook.com/nybeachrepublic; Hat Nai Yang; ⊙from 3pm; 🛜)

Northern Beaches Eating & Drinking

Hat Mai Khao (p131)

Worth a Trip 🔭
Hidden Hôrng of Ao Phang-Nga

Between turquoise bays peppered with craggy limestone towers, sparkling white beaches and tumble-down fishing villages, Ao Phang-Nga makes up one of Thailand's most majestic landscapes. The bay may be swarming with tour groups in motorboats year-round, but once you start navigating its soul-stirring scenery and soaking up the tranquil confines of its famous hôrng (semi-submerged island lagoons), awe inevitably descends.

⚓ Day trip with Phuket-based operator (from 3500B).

⚓ In Phang-Nga Province, charter boats from Tha Dan, 9km south of Phang-Nga (from 1500B), or go with a local tour company.

Ao Phang-Nga National Park

Famous for its glorious castle-like karst scenery, Ao Phang-Nga's 400-sq-km **marine national park** (อุทยานแห่งชาติอ่าวพังงา; ☏076 481188; www.dnp.go.th; adult/child 300/100B; ⏰8am-4.30pm) was established in 1981. It was created by mainland fault movements pushing massive limestone rocks into geometric patterns. These blocks extended southward into Ao Phang-Nga, forming 42 islands marked by sheer towering cliffs and caves opening up hidden *hôrng*. The bay itself is made up of tidal channels that run north to south through Thailand's largest remaining primary mangrove forests. The best way to visit is by kayak, SUP or long-tail boat tour.

Hôrng by Starlight

Slip through pitch-black bat caves into secluded *hôrng*: lagoons protected by limestone cliffs that tower out of the sea. Along the way you'll be accompanied by sea eagles, and you may spot monkeys, pythons and monitor lizards. Reputable and ecologically sensitive, **John Gray's Sea-canoe** (☏076 254505; www.johngray-seacanoe.com; 86 Soi 2/3, Th Yaowarat; adult/child from 3950/1975B) was the first kayak outfitter in the bay; the 'Hong by Starlight' trip dodges the crowds, with sunset dinner and an introduction to Ao Phang-Nga's celebrated after-dark bioluminescence.

The Islands

Ao Phang-Nga National Park's major tourist drawcard is the perpetually photographed, geographically spectacular **Ko Khao Phing Kan** (เกาะเขาพิงกัน, James Bond Island), which once starred in *The Man with the Golden Gun* (1974); today it's crammed with day trippers and vendors flogging coral and shells that would be better off in the sea. The small, much-visited karst island of **Ko Panyi** (เกาะปันหยี) is home to a stilted Muslim fishing village. You can spend the night there for a more peaceful experience.

★ Top Tips

∘ Explore in the early morning, stay out for the evening and/or arrange your own transport to sidestep the crowds.

∘ Stay overnight in simple accommodation on Ko Panyi to soak up the stunning scenery without interruptions.

∘ Pack your hat, swimsuit, sunnies and sunscreen.

∘ At the time of writing, there were plans to introduce compulsory advanced e-ticketing for the national park: watch this space.

✕ Take a Break

Most tours include a straightforward Thai meal with water and soft drinks.

Worth a Trip 🔭
Diving in the Similan Islands

Famous among divers, the 70-sq-km Similan Islands Marine National Park is Thailand's premier dive spot. Its granite islands, 70km offshore from Phang-Nga Province and 90km northwest of Phuket, wow with turquoise water and kaleidoscopic corals, fringed by rainforest and silky soft white beaches. Coral bleaching has killed many hard corals and overtourism is a serious concern, but the soft corals and wildlife are still here.

อุทยานแห่งชาติ
หมู่เกาะสิมิลัน

📞 076 453272

www.dnp.go.th

adult/child 500/300B

🕑 mid-Oct–mid-May

Going Underwater

With dramatic underwater gorges and boulder swim-throughs, the Similans cater to all diving levels, at depths of 2m to 30m. You'll find dive sites at the islands north of **Ko Miang**; the park's southern section (Islands 1, 2 and 3) is an off-limits turtle-nesting ground.

Ko Hin Pousar (เกาะหินพูซ่า, Island 7) has rock reefs and there are dive-throughs at **Hin Pousar** (หินพูซ่า, Elephant Head Rock); plume worms, soft corals, schooling fish, manta rays and rare whale sharks are among the local marine life. **Ko Bon** (เกาะบอน), largely unscathed by coral bleaching, is Thailand's prime manta-ray dive site. **Ko Tachai** (เกาะตาชัย), was closed to day trippers in 2016 due to environmental concerns, though dive boats can still do dives here.

Hiking

The forest around Ko Miang's **visitors centre** (Ko Miang/Island 4; ⏱7.30am-8pm mid-Oct–mid May) has some walking trails and great wildlife, starting with a small 400m beach track to a little snorkelling bay. If you detour from here, the **Viewpoint Trail** unveils panoramic vistas after 30 minutes of steep scrambling. A 20-minute forest walk west from the visitors centre leads to a smooth west-facing granite platform, **Sunset Point** (แหลมซันเซ็ท).

On **Ko Similan** (เกาะสิมิลัน; Island 8), you can hike 2.5km through the forest to a **viewpoint** (จุดชมวิว เกาะสิมิลัน), and scramble up from the north-coast beach to **Sail Rock** (หินเรือใบ, Balance Rock); during daylight it's clogged with visitors.

Wildlife

The fabulous Nicobar pigeon, with its wild mane of grey-green feathers, is endemic to the islands of the Andaman Sea and one of the park's 39 bird species. Hairy-legged land crabs, flying squirrels and fruit bats (flying foxes) are relatively easy to spot amid the forest.

★ **Top Tips**

o The Similans close from mid-May to mid-October.

o Overnight stays on the islands are banned, though divers can stay the night on a liveaboard.

o Unmonitored tourism is damaging the park. Tread lightly; don't feed fish.

o February to April has top visibility.

o At the time of writing, an obligatory advance e-ticket system for the national park is expected to be implemented.

o The park **headquarters** (Mu 5, Thap Lamu; ⏱8am-5pm) is 12km south of Khao Lak on the mainland.

✕ **Take a Break**

All tours and liveaboards include simple meals, drinking water and soft drinks.

★ **Getting There**

⚓ Day tours, two-dive day trips and multiday liveaboards from Phuket or Khao Lak are the only ways to access the Similans.

Worth a Trip 👀
Ko Phi-Phi Day Trip

With bleach-blonde beaches, bodacious jungles and long-tail boats puttering between craggy cliffs rising from brilliantly turquoise waters, the insanely beautiful national-park islands of Ko Phi-Phi Don and Ko Phi-Phi Leh feel like tropical-isle clichés turned stunning reality. Their immense popularity, however, is taking a serious toll on the delicate local environment, and can leave visitors shocked and underwhelmed: tread lightly.

Ko Phi-Phi is 47km south-east of Phuket.

⚓ Boats leave Phuket's Tha Rassada at 8.30am, 11am, 12.20pm and 1.30pm, returning at 9am, 11am, 2.30pm and 3.30pm (from 300B, two hours).

Diving & Snorkelling

Phi-Phi's crystalline waters and abundant marine life make for top-notch scuba diving. Popular dive sites include **King Cruiser Wreck** (ซากเรือคิงครูยเซอร์); **Anemone Reef**; **Hin Bida Phi-Phi**; **Ko Bida Nok** (เกาะบิดานอก), attracting leopard sharks; and **Kledkaeo Wreck** (ซากเรือเกล็ดแก้ว).

There are a number of reliable Phuket-based dive operators (p17). Ko Phi-Phi's **Adventure Club** (☎081 970 0314; www.diving-in thailand. net; 125/19 Mu 7, Ton Sai Village; 2-dive trip 2500B; ⏰7am-10pm) is a responsible outfit.

Ko Mai Phai, 6km north of Phi-Phi Don, is a popular shallow snorkelling spot home to small sharks. You'll find more good snorkelling along the eastern coast of **Ko Nok** (near Ao Ton Sai), along the eastern coast of **Ko Nai**, and off **Hat Yao**. Snorkelling trips cost 600B to 1500B, excluding national-park fees. Many dive schools offer specialised snorkelling tours or tag-along prices for snorkellers.

Phi-Phi Viewpoint

A tough 20- to 30-minute climb, up hundreds of steps and narrow paths from Ton Sai Village to **Phi-Phi Viewpoint** (จุดชมวิวเกาะพีพีดอน; 30B), is rewarded with exquisite views of Ko Phi Phi's lush mountainous brilliance.

Ko Phi-Phi Leh

Ko Phi-Phi Leh has been a popular site since *The Beach* was filmed here, especially beautiful **Ao Maya** (อ่าวมาหยา; Maya Bay). The overwhelming mass tourism is devastating Phi-Phi Leh's ecosystem. An estimated 80% of Ao Maya's coral has been destroyed, leading Thai authorities to close the bay indefinitely in 2018 to allow for regeneration. Many environmentalists, however, have expressed concerns that the islands' preservation requires more long-term measures.

★ **Top Tips**

o Phi-Phi's fragile ecosystem and infrastructure is struggling to cope with the endless influx of tourists; leave as little impact as possible.

o National-park admission fees are 400/200B per foreign adult/child, plus 200B per diver. At the time of writing, obligatory advance e-tickets for are expected to be introduced.

o Arrive at Tha Rassada early to bag a good lounging spot for the boat ride over.

✕ **Take a Break**

Feast on Mediterranean delights at Turkish Ton Sai Village restaurant **Efe** (☎095 150 4434; www.facebook.com/ eferestaurant; mains 170-600B; ⏰noon-10.30pm; 📶).

For global bites and cocktails, hunt down expat fave **Unni's** (☎091 837 5931; www. facebook.com/unnis. phiphi; Ton Sai Village, Ko Phi-Phi Don; mains 140-600B; ⏰8am-11pm; 📶).

Survival Guide

Travelling via túk-túk (p148) AKHENATON IMAGES/SHUTTERSTOCK ©

Before You Go

Book Your Stay

Book well in advance from November to April. Outside these months, Phuket remains busy but room prices drop by up to 50%.

Hotels From chic boutique revamps of Phuket Town's Sino-Portuguese buildings to some of Thailand's most luxurious beach resorts.

Hostels Phuket's flourishing hostel scene centres on affordable Phuket Town and pricier Patong; also good options in Kata, Karon and Ao Bang Thao.

Guesthouses Small, good-value operations with more character than their hotel competitors.

Apartments Handy for anyone in a group; easily booked through rental websites including Airbnb.

Best Budget

Fin Hostel (☎ 088 753 1162; www.finhostelphuket. com; 100/20 Th Kata/

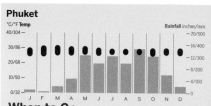

Phuket

°C/°F Temp — Rainfall inches/mm

When to Go

High Season (Dec–Feb) Blue skies and calm seas post-monsoon. Prices and crowds soar; book accommodation well ahead.

Shoulder (Nov & Mar–Apr) Weather is a good bet; average temperatures of 31°C. Still some crowds, but without peak accommodation rates.

Low Season (May–Oct) Phuket's humid monsoon; expect rain and rougher seas, but also some sun. Great accommodation discounts (often 50%). Vegetarian Festival (September/October).

Patak West; dm 300-600B, capsules 300-1000B, d 1500-3000B; ❄ 🛜 🏊) Gleaming bunks, capsules and private rooms in Kata.

Lub*d (☎ 076 530100; www.lubd.com; 5/5 Th Sawatdirak; incl breakfast dm 650B, d 2600-3200B; @ 🛜 🏊) Sociable, stylish hostel in party-mad Patong.

Ai Phuket Hostel (☎ 076 212881; www.aiphukethostel.com; 88 Th Yaowarat; dm 279B, d 600-900B; ❄ @ 🛜) Popular Phuket Town budget pick.

ChillHub Hostel (☎ 082 291 1925; www.facebook.com/chillhub phukethostel; 69/140-142 Mu 3, Hat Bang Thao; dm 500-600B; ❄ 🛜 🏊) Crisply contemporary hostel in Bang Thao.

Art-C House (☎ 082 420 3911; www.facebook.com/artchouse; 288 Th Phuket; d 800B; 🛜) Original murals, good-value rooms. In Phuket Town.

Doolay Hostel (☎ 062 451 9546; www.doolay hostel.com; 164 Th Karon/Patak West; dm 600B; ❄ 🛜) Modern beach-facing Karon hostel.

Best Midrange

Casa Blanca Boutique Hotel (076 219019; www.casablancaphuket.com; 26 Th Phuket; d 2300-2800B; ❄ @ ☎) Spanish inspiration meets Sino-Portuguese character in Phuket Town.

PapaCrab (076 385315; www.phuketpapacrab.com; 93/5 Mu 3, Th Rim Hat; d 1900-2300B; ☺Oct-Jul; ❄ ☎) Cosy boutique-inspired Kamala base run by on-the-ball owners.

RomManee (089 728 9871; Soi Romanee; d 1200B; ❄ ☎) Stylish boutique guesthouse behind a Sino-Portuguese facade on Phuket Town's prettiest street.

Sabai Corner (089 875 5525; www.sabaicornerphuket.com; Soi Laem Mum Nai, off Rte 4233; d 1500B; P ☎) Fabulous 270-degree ocean views from isolated, fan-cooled hillside chalets, between Kata and Rawai.

Baan Suwantawe (076 212879; www.baansuwantawe.com; 11/9-10 Th Dibuk; d 1700-3000B; P ❄ ☎) Excellent-value studio-style rooms with charming modern-Thai decor, overlooking

a pool in Phuket Town.

Benyada Lodge (081 889 4173; www.benyadalodge-phuket.com; 106/52 Mu 3; d incl breakfast 2800-4500B; ❄ @ ☎) Comfy colourful hotel with contemporary flair, just back from Hat Surin.

Best Top End

Keemala (076 358777; www.keemala.com; 10/88 Mu 6, Th Nakasod; villas incl breakfast 22,200-31,600B; P ❄ ☎) Eco-conscious, fantasy-inspired Kamala spa resort.

Sri Panwa (076 371000; www.sripanwa.com; 88 Mu 8, Th Sak-didej; incl breakfast ste 13,700-24,000B, 1-room villas 21,300-31,000B;

P ❄ ☎) Luxury hotel on Phuket's spectacular Laem Phanwa.

Surin Phuket (076 316400; www.thesurinphuket.com; 118 Mu 3; d incl breakfast 11,000-40,000B; P ❄ ☎) Top-end Surin resort overlooking peaceful Hat Pansea.

Anantara Phuket Layan (076 317200; www.anantara.com; 168 Mu 6, Soi 4; incl breakfast d 10,140-15,780B, 1-bedroom villas 11,820-38,450B; P ❄ ☎) Private-pool villas with open-air bathtubs on Hat Layan.

Amanpuri Resort (076 324333; www.aman.com; Hat Pansea; 1-bedroom villas incl breakfast US$1200-4000;

P ❄ 🛜 ✈) The queen of Phuket's exclusive hotels.

Point Yamu by Como

(📞 076 360100; www. comohotels.com; 225 Mu 7, Paklok, Laem Yamu; d incl breakfast 10,600-32,200B; P ❄ 🛜 ✈) A Laem Yamu stunner blending Thai influences with Italian design.

Arriving in Phuket

Phuket International Airport

Phuket International Airport (www.phuket airportonline.com) is 30km northwest of Phuket Town. THAI flies to/from Bangkok (Suvarnabhumi); AirAsia, Nok Air and Bangkok Airways all serve Bangkok, plus other national destinations. Direct international destinations include Hong Kong, Kuala Lumpur, Singapore, Beijing, Shanghai, Seoul, Delhi, Mumbai, Sydney and the Gulf States.

Bus Twelve daily orange government airport buses (www.airportbus phuket.com) run between the airport and Phuket Town's **Bus Terminal 1** (Th Phang-Nga) (100B, one hour), leaving the airport from 8am to 8.30pm and Phuket Town from 6am to 6.30pm.

Phuket Smart Bus (📞 086 306 1257; www. phuketsmartbus.com; 50-170B) travels from the airport to Rawai via the west-coast beaches and back.

Taxi Metered taxis are just left outside of the international arrivals hall; rates shouldn't be more than 700B.

Minivan To west-coast beaches (200B).

Tha Rassada & Tha Bang Rong

o Phuket's Tha Rassada, 3km southeast of Phuket Town, is the main pier for boats to/from Ko Phi-Phi, Krabi, Ao Nang, Ko Lanta, the Trang Islands, Ko Lipe and even as far as Pulau Langkawi in Malaysia.

Marine Environment & Responsible Travel

It's hard to ignore the rubbish on Phuket's beaches these days. That said, things have been slowly improving since the Phuket beach clean-up kicked off in 2014. On Phuket's heavily touristed Coral Island, 75% of coral reefs have been destroyed in the last 10 years, leading to emergency measures being announced in 2017. Ko Phi-Phi Leh's immensely popular Ao Maya closed completely to visitors indefinitely in 2018 to allow it to recover from overtourism.

Phuket generates an average of 850 tonnes of rubbish each day. Do your bit by throwing your rubbish in the bin, picking up other debris wherever you can, and avoiding the use of plastic bottles, bags and straws. Local beach clean-up projects, such as those run by **Trash Hero Phuket** (www.facebook.com/TrashHeroPhuket), are always in need of volunteers. When swimming, diving or snorkelling, do not touch or walk on coral, and do not harass marine life.

Phuket Taxis

Despite crackdowns on Phuket's 'taxi mafia' by the Thai military, taxis remain seriously overpriced across the island. A 15-minute journey from, say, Hat Karon to Hat Patong will set you back 400B. Price boards around the island outline *maximum* journey rates, though drivers rarely budge from them.

To avoid being overcharged, jot down the phone number of a metered taxi and use the same driver throughout your stay. The best way to do this is to take a metered taxi from the airport (the easiest place to find them) when you arrive. Set rates are 50B for the first 2km, 12B per kilometre for the next 15km and 10B per kilometre thereafter, plus a 100B 'airport tax'.

The popular Grab taxi app (www.grab.com) is very handy on Phuket. Taxis booked via Grab use meters and add a small pick-up charge, though they aren't always cheaper than taxis hailed on the street. Grab drivers may not understand English, but your accommodation can help.

o Additional services to Krabi and Ao Nang via the Ko Yao Islands leave from Tha Bang Rong, 26km north of Tha Rassada.

Phuket Bus Terminal 2

o Interstate buses depart from **Phuket Bus Terminal 2** (Th Thepkrasattri), 4km north of Phuket Town. Destinations include Bangkok, Chiang Mai, Chiang Rai, Hat Yai, Ko Samui, Ko Pha-Ngan and Surat Thani.

Phuket Bus Terminal 1

o Phuket travel agencies sell tickets (including ferry fare) for shared air-con minivans to destinations across southern Thailand, including Krabi, Ranong, Trang, Surat Thani, Ko Samui, Ko Pha-Ngan and Hat Yai. Prices are usually slightly higher than for buses. Many minivans use **Phuket Bus Terminal 1** (Th Phang-Nga) in Phuket Town.

Getting Around

Car & Motorcycle

o Motorbike hire costs around 250B per day across the island.

o You can rent cars pretty much anywhere – including at the airport and in Phuket Town – from around 1000B per day. Reliable operators include **Andaman Car Rent** (076 621600; www.andamancarrent.com; 112/12 Mu 3; 9am-7pm), **Avis** (089 969 8674; www.avis.com; Phuket International Airport; 7am-midnight), **Hertz** (076 328545; www.hertz.com; Phuket International Airport; 24hr) and **Pure Car Rent** (076 211002; www.purecarrent.com; 73 Th Rassada; 9am-7pm).

Bus

o Launched in 2018, the sky-blue **Phuket Smart**

Gibbon Poaching

Gibbon poaching is a big problem on Phuket, fuelled in no small part by tourism: captive gibbons are paraded around tourist bars and beaches as photo ops. Phuket's last wild white-handed gibbon was poached in the early 1980s. You can help by not having your photo taken with Phuket's captive gibbons and by supporting the **Phuket Gibbon Rehabilitation Project** (p125).

Bus (📞 086 306 1257; www.phuketsmartbus.com; 50-170B) runs between Phuket airport and Rawai (two hours) via Ao Bang Thao, Surin, Kamala, Patong, Karon and Kata roughly hourly from 6am to 8.15pm.

○ Rates are 50B to 170B You'll need a prepaid smartcard (300B), which can be bought on board and topped up at designated spots across the island.

○ There's an hourly Smart Night Bus (150B) from 9pm to 2am between Kamala and Kata via Patong and Karon.

Sŏrng·tăa·ou & Túk-Túk

○ Large bus-sized *sŏrng·tăa·ou* (passenger pick-up trucks) run regularly between Th Ranong in Phuket Town and most of the beaches (30B to 40B, 30 minutes to 1½ hours), from 7am to 5pm or 6pm.

○ Túk-túk charters are another way to get around.

Boat

○ Long-tail and speed-boat charters are handy for visiting outlying islands, especially from Rawai.

Essential Information

Accessible Travel

Phuket (like most of Thailand) is an ongoing obstacle course for the mobility impaired, with high kerbs, uneven footpaths, nonstop traffic and a shortage of ramps or other access points for wheelchairs. That said, some of the island's top-end hotels make consistent efforts to provide disabled access, while other hotels with high employee-to-guest ratios are usually good about accommodating the mobility impaired. For the rest, you're pretty much left to your own resources, so advance planning will be essential.

○ Specialised travel agent Phuket Access Travel (www.phuketaccesstravel.com), founded by a team with personal experience of disability, offers wheelchair-accessible transport, as well as beach wheelchairs, accommodation recommendations and adapted tours (including to Big Buddha, Hat Nai Han and Laem Phromthep).

○ You'll find hotel recommendations through reputable Disabled Holidays (www.disabledholidays.com).

○ Download Lonely Planet's free Accessible Travel guides from http://lptravel.to/Accessible-Travel.

The Plight of Phuket's Elephants

Although you don't have to travel far to meet Phuket's majestic elephants, the encounters on offer (rides, photo shoots, circus-like 'performances') are associated with complex animal-welfare issues. There is now overwhelming evidence of the serious harm that unnatural human-elephant interactions cause to these empathetic, sociable and highly intelligent creatures.

Illegal capture and trade to fuel the tourism industry are major threats to Thailand's dwindling wild-elephant population: only around 1800 remain in the wild; an additional 3000 to 4000 are 'domesticated'. Many just-captured and captive-born elephants undergo a brutal process of being 'crushed' into submission via repetitive physical and psychological abuse. Phuket is home to 235 officially registered elephants, most of which 'work' in camps.

Although trekking isn't inherently harmful to elephants, overloading their spines is. Experts indicate that adult elephants can comfortably carry up to 150kg at a time, for up to four hours a day; these limits are seriously exceeded at high-demand trekking camps. Many experts insist that rides should be entirely avoided, due to the brutal abuse elephants are subjected to to 'learn' how to carry riders. Bathing with elephants is also harmful, warn experts, as it's unnatural behaviour.

While boycotting elephant camps might seem like the obvious solution, the situation is complicated. Without tourist demand, and with Thailand's few responsible sanctuaries currently unable to take in all of the country's mahouts and their charges, mahouts claim they (and their elephants) will have no source of income.

Phuket (along with the rest of Thailand) is slowly experiencing a rise in demand for more responsible elephant encounters, spearheaded by the pioneering ethical **Phuket Elephant Sanctuary** (p127; linked to Chiang Mai's respected Elephant Nature Park). Some Phuket operators are beginning to look towards this model in finding a balance between the needs of elephants, mahouts and tourists, but there's a long way to go. Others, however, are leaping on the 'sanctuary' bandwagon without taking any responsible steps. Avoid outfits that involve shows, tricks, trekking and other unnatural behaviour; lack sufficient water, shade or food; or use bull-hooks and/or chains.

Largely due to mounting international pressure, Thailand is working on improving conditions for its captive elephants and cracking down on elephant-smuggling across the Myanmar border. As of 2016, all captive elephants must be registered on a central DNA database within 90 days of birth – thus (hopefully) preventing the illegal introduction of newly captured elephants into Thai camps.

Electricity

Type A
220V/50Hz

Type C
220V/50Hz

Business Hours

Banks and government offices close for national holidays. Some bars and clubs close during elections and certain religious holidays when alcohol sales are banned.

Banks 8.30am–4.30pm; 24-hour ATMs

Bars 6pm–midnight or 1am; **Clubs** 8pm–2am

Government offices 8.30am–4.30pm Monday to Friday; some close for lunch

Restaurants 8am–10pm

Shops 10am–7pm

Emergencies

Thailand's country code	☎66
International access codes	☎001, ☎007, ☎008, ☎009 (& other promotional codes)
Operator-assisted international calls	☎100
Emergency	☎191
Tourist police	☎1155

LGBT+ Travellers

Thai culture is relatively tolerant of both male and female homosexuality. There is a fairly prominent LGBT+ scene in Bangkok, Pattaya and Phuket, with Phuket hosting Thailand's top **Pride Week** (www.phuket-pride.org) every year in April.

With regard to dress or mannerism, the LGBT+ community is generally accepted without comment. However, public displays of affection – whether heterosexual or homosexual – are frowned upon.

Utopia (www.utopia-asia.com) and Gay Patong (www.gaypatong.com) are helpful resources for LGBT+ travellers. Phuket's (predominantly male) LGBT+ scene centres on Patong's Royal Paradise Complex.

Money

Most places in Thailand deal only with cash. Some credit and debit cards are accepted in high-end establishments. The local currency is Thai baht (B).

ATMs

o Debit and credit cards issued in your own country can be used at

ATMs across Phuket to withdraw cash (in Thai baht only).

○ Most ATMs allow a maximum of 20,000B in withdrawals per day, and charge a 200B foreign-transaction fee.

Tipping

○ Tipping is not generally expected in Thailand, though it is appreciated. It is fairly common to leave the loose change from a large restaurant bill.

○ At many hotel restaurants and upmarket eateries, a 10% service charge will be added to your bill.

Public Holidays

Government offices and banks close their doors on the following public holidays. For the precise dates of lunar holidays, see the Events & Festivals page of the Tourism Authority of Thailand website (www.tourismthailand.org/Events-and-Festivals).

1 January New Year's Day

February (date varies) Makha Bucha; Buddhist holy day

Phuket Media

Blogs Good English-language blogs about Phuket include *Jamie's Phuket* (www.jamiesphuketblog.com), *Phuket 101* (www.phuket101.net) and *Go Phuket* (www.gophuket.net).

News Local English-language news media: *The Phuket News* (www.thephuketnews.com), and *The Thaiger* (www.thethaiger.com). Thailand-wide, there's *Bangkok Post* (www.bangkokpost.com), business-heavy *Nation* (www.nationmultimedia.com) and *KhaoSod English* (www.khaosodenglish.com), the English-language service of a mainstream Thai newspaper.

6 April Chakri Day; commemorating the founder of the Chakri dynasty, Rama I

13–15 April Songkran Festival

1 May Labour Day

5 May Coronation Day

May/June (date varies) Visakha Bucha; Buddhist holy day

28 July King Maha Vajiralongkorn's Birthday

July/August (date varies) Asanha Bucha; Buddhist holy day

12 August Queen Sirikit's Birthday/Mother's Day

23 October Chulalongkorn Day

5 December Commemoration of Late King Bhumibol/Father's Day

10 December Constitution Day

31 December New Year's Eve

Safe Travel

○ Thousands of people are injured or killed yearly on Phuket's highways.

○ Take special care on the roads from Patong to Karon and from Kata to Rawai/Hat Nai Han: we've had reports of late-night motorbike muggings and stabbings.

○ Sunbathing topless is a big no-no in Thailand for women.

○ Drownings occur every year off Phuket's beaches; take care (p152).

o Drug possession can result in a year or more of prison. Drug smuggling carries considerably higher penalties, including execution.

o Jet-ski scams (p60) plague Phuket; inspect before hiring.

o There have been serious boat accidents; ensure your boat has safety/emergency equipment; if in doubt, find another operator.

Beach Safety

o During the May–October monsoon, large waves and fierce undertows can make swimming dangerous.

Dozens of drownings occur every year on Phuket's beaches, especially Laem Singh, Kamala, Karon and Patong. Heed the red flags signalling a serious rip.

o At any time of year, keep an eye out for jet skis and long-tail boats when swimming; do not expect drivers/boatmen to see you!

Smoking

o Banned in Thai restaurants and bars since 2008, and on some Thai beaches (including Patong) since 2018.

Telephone

o The telephone country code for Thailand is 66 and is used when calling the country from abroad.

o All Thai telephone numbers are preceded by a '0' if you're dialling domestically (the '0' is omitted when calling from overseas). After the initial '0', the next two numbers represent the provincial area code, which is now integral to the telephone number; Phuket's provincial code is 76.

o If the initial '0' is followed by a '6', an '8' or a '9', you're dialling a mobile phone.

Dos & Don'ts

Thais are generally very understanding and hospitable, but there are some important taboos and social conventions (even on touristed Phuket).

Monarchy It is a criminal offence to disrespect the royal family; treat objects depicting the king (like money) with respect.

Temples Wear clothing that covers to your knees and elbows. Remove all footwear before entering. Sit with your feet tucked behind you, so they are not facing the Buddha image. Women should never touch a monk or a monk's belongings; step out of the way and don't sit next to them.

Modesty At the beach, avoid public nudity or topless sunbathing. Cover up going to and from the beach.

Body language Avoid touching anyone on the head and be careful where you point your feet; they're the lowest part of the body.

Saving face The best way to win over the Thais is to smile; visible anger or arguing is embarrassing.

Mobile Phones

The easiest option is to acquire a mobile phone equipped with a local SIM card. Prepaid SIM cards can be easily purchased. SIM cards include talk and data packages and you can add more funds with a prepaid reload card.

Toilets

Across Thailand the Western-style toilet is becoming more prevalent than the squat toilet and appears wherever foreign tourists can be found, including Phuket. That said, the septic system may not be designed to take toilet paper; in such cases there will be a waste basket.

Tourist Information

You'll find tourist information offices in Phuket Town.

Tourism Authority of Thailand (TAT; ☎ 076 211036; www.tourism thailand.org/Phuket; 191 Th Thalang; ⏰ 8.30am-4.30pm)

Tourist Information Centre (Th Thalang; ⏰ 9am-10pm)

Visas

○ For visitors from most countries, visas are generally not required for stays of up to 30 days. For some nationalities, 15 days rather than 30 days is given if arriving by land rather than air.

○ Without proof of an onward ticket and sufficient funds for your projected stay, you can be denied entry, but in practice this formality is rarely checked.

○ The **Ministry of Foreign Affairs** (☎ 02 203 5000; www.mfa.go.th) oversees immigration and visa issues. The best online monitor of changes in regulations is Thaivisa (www.thaivisa. com).

Language

In Thai the meaning of a syllable may be altered by means of tones. Standard Thai has five tones: low (eg bàht), mid (eg dee), falling (eg mâi), high (eg máh) and rising (eg sǎhm).

Read our pronunciation guides as if they were English and you'll be understood.

Basics

Hello.	สวัสดี	sà-wàt-dee
Goodbye.	ลาก่อน	lah gòrn
Yes./No.	ใช่/ไม่	châi/mâi
Please.	ขอ	kǒr
Thank you.	ขอบคุณ	kòrp kun
Excuse me.	ขออภัย	kǒr à-pai
Sorry.	ขอโทษ	kǒr tôht

Eating & Drinking

I'd like (the menu), please.

ขอ (รายการ อาหาร) หน่อย — kǒr (rai gahn ah-hǎhn) nòy

Cheers!

ไชโย — chai-yoh

Please bring the bill.

ขอบิลหน่อย — kǒr bin nòy

Shopping

I'd like to buy ...

อยากจะซื้อ ... — yàhk jà séu ...

How much is it?

เท่าไร — tôw-rai

Can you lower the price?

ลดราคาได้ไหม — lót rah-kah dâi mǎi

Emergencies

Help!	ช่วยด้วย	chôo·ay dôo·ay
Go away!	ไปให้พ้น	bai hâi pón

Call a doctor!

เรียกหมอหน่อย — rêe·ak mǒr nòy

Call the police!

เรียกตำรวจหน่อย — rêe·ak đam·ròo·at nòy

I'm ill.

ผม/ดิฉัน — pǒm/dì-chǎn
ป่วย — bòo·ay (m/f)

I'm lost.

ผม/ดิฉัน — pǒm/dì-chǎn
หลงทาง — lǒng tahng (m/f)

Where are the toilets?

ห้องน้ำอยู่ที่ไหน — hôrng nám yòo têe nǎi

Transport & Directions

Where's ...?

... อยู่ที่ไหน — ... yòo têe nǎi

Can you show me (on the map)?

ให้ดู (ในแผนที่) — hâi doo (nai pǎen têe)
ได้ไหม — dâi mǎi

Index

Sights 000
Map Pages **000**

Behind the Scenes

Send Us Your Feedback

We love to hear from travellers – your comments help make our books better. We read every word, and we guarantee that your feedback goes straight to the authors. Visit **lonelyplanet.com/contact** to submit your updates and suggestions.

Note: We may edit, reproduce and incorporate your comments in Lonely Planet products such as guidebooks, websites and digital products, so let us know if you don't want your comments reproduced or your name acknowledged. For a copy of our privacy policy visit lonelyplanet.com/privacy.

Isabella's Thanks

The biggest *kòrp kun ka* to Tash Eldred, Noi Tammasak, Louis Kettle, Meri Hoffsten, Alessandro Frau, Natt Suttichada, Lee Cobaj, Pimkan Kongsanoon, Ashley Niedringhaus, Wiwan Bumrungwong, Amy Bensema, Jamie Monk and Charly Hegret for all things Phuket. Back home, thanks to Jack, Paps, Don, Sarah, Andrew and my fab writer friends.

Acknowledgements

Cover photograph: Long-tail boat on Andaman beach, Kittikorn Nimitpara/Getty©

This Book

This 5th edition of Lonely Planet's *Pocket Phuket* guidebook was researched and written by Isabella Noble. The previous edition was also written by Isabella. This guidebook was produced by the following:

Destination Editor
Tanya Parker

Senior Product Editor
Kate Chapman

Regional Senior Cartographer
Diana Von Holdt

Product Editor
Amy Lynch

Book Designer
Virginia Moreno

Assisting Editors
Kellie Langdon, Kristin Odijk

Assisting Cartographer
Mark Griffiths

Cover Researcher
Meri Blazevski

Thanks to
Ronan Abayawickrema, Gwen Cotter, Martin Heng, Alicia Johnson, Sandie Kestell, Karyn Noble, Claire Naylor, Genna Patterson, Deepabali Roy, Eleanor Simpson, James Smart

Our Writer

Isabella Noble

English-Australian on paper but Spanish at heart, Isabella has been wandering the globe since her fir round-the-world trip as a one-year-old. Having grow up in a whitewashed Andalucian village, she is a Sp specialist travel journalist, but also writes extensive about India, Thailand, the UK and beyond for Lonel Planet, the *Daily Telegraph* and others. Isabella has co-written Lonely Planet guides to *Spain* and *Anda-lucía*, and is a *Daily Telegraph* Spain expert. She has also contributed to Lonely Planet *India*, *South India Thailand*, *Thailand's Islands & Beaches*, *Southeast Asia on a Shoestring* and *Great Britain*, and authore *Pocket Phuket*. Find Isabella on Twitter and Instagra (@isabellamnoble).

Published by Lonely Planet Global Limited
CRN 554153
5th edition – July 2019
ISBN 978 1 78657 478 7
© Lonely Planet 2019 Photographs © as indicated 2019
10 9 8 7 6 5 4 3 2 1
Printed in Singapore

Although the authors and Lonely Planet have taken all reasonable care in preparin this book, we make no warranty about the accuracy or completeness of its content a to the maximum extent permitted, disclai all liability arising from its use.